THE APPRENTICE

SIR ALAN SUGAR

BOOKS

HOW TO GET HIRED NOT FIRED

SIR ALAN SUGAR

BOOKS

To accompany the Talkback series produced for BBC TV

**Sir Alan Sugar is donating all his earnings
from sales of *The Apprentice* to charity.**

Published by BBC Books, BBC Worldwide Limited,
Woodlands, 80 Wood Lane, London W12 0TT

First published 2005 by BBC Worldwide Limited to accompany the Talkback series
produced for BBC TV.

© Talkback (UK) Productions Limited, 2005
The moral right of the author has been asserted.

ISBN: 0 563 52238 0

Senior Commissioning Editor: Nicky Ross
Editor and Researcher: Sarah Sutton
Project Editor: Charlotte Lochhead
Copy Editor: Patricia Burgess
Designer: Ann Burnham
Production Controller: Kenneth McKay
Photographs © James Bainbridge
(pages 14-15, 32, 64, 134) and Adam Lawrence
© BBC/Talkback Thames

Set in Frutiger and Walbaum
Printed and bound in Great Britain by CPI Bath

For more information about this and other BBC books,
please call 08700 777 001 or visit our website on www.bbcshop.co.uk

Acknowledgements

This book could not have been written without the enthusiasm and assistance of the team at Talkback. Particular thanks go to Cat Ledger for making it all possible, and to Peter Moore, Tanya Shaw, Dan Adamson, Charlotte Wasserman, Alf Lawrie, James Bainbridge, Sophie Leonard, Emma Riley and Beth Dicks, without whom the very tight deadline would never have been met. In addition, I would like to thank all the Apprentices for their enthusiasm, dedication and willingness to undertake all the tasks. Thanks to Sarah Sutton for putting the words on the page and also to Keith King for his knowledge and support.

The team at BBC Worldwide have done a highly professional job in delivering this book to market in a way worthy of *The Apprentice*. Under the creative and focused leadership of Nicky Ross, Senior Commissioning Editor, Charlotte Lochhead overcame several challenges as Project Editor and with Trish Burgess, Ann Burnham and Ken McKay delivered the final product on time.

Amongst my own highly respected team of colleagues and advisors I would like to acknowledge the professional help and involvement of my eyes and ears: Margaret Mountford and Nick Hewer; as well as my expert advisors: Bordan Tkachuk, CEO of Viglen, Claude Littner, Amstrad Group Advisor, and Paul Kemsley, founding director of Rock Investments. I'd also like to acknowledge the support and enthusiasm of my wife, Ann, who tolerated my absence over an extended period of time during the filming.

I'm glad to say no one was fired!

Contents

WANTED

---

for *THE APPRENTICE*

Ambitious and hungry individuals:
Britain's brightest young business minds

Seven men – Seven women – One prize

All the winner has to do is survive
12 business tasks in the longest and most
exhilarating job interview ever.

REWARD

In exchange for demonstrating skill, talent,
motivation and business acumen, the winner
will get the chance to
**work for one year as The Apprentice to
Sir Alan Sugar**
and to
earn a six-figure salary
working at the helm of one of his companies.

INTRODUCTION

Have you got what it takes?

The Apprentice began as a ground-breaking television programme, but I want it to bring out the entrepreneurial skills in every aspiring business pioneer. *The Apprentice* offers a virtual apprenticeship to business professionals and entrepreneurs alike.

I've been in business since I was a 12-year-old school kid really. If there was an opportunity and a demand I'd be there. It was an instinct, and gave me a buzz that has never left me. There are plenty of other young Sugars out there, and I want to help them to succeed.

The UK television series of *The Apprentice* has its roots in the USA, where a highly successful show of the same name, hosted by Donald Trump, was watched by millions of people. The show broke the mould of so-called 'reality' TV shows because it focused on the world of business. In the UK version we began with a team of fourteen candidates who were whittled down to a single finalist over a twelve-week period. I was looking for someone with an eye for profit, a mind for new ideas, a flexibility of approach and a buzz of energy that meant they'd be hungry to help me build a successful business. The interview process was created around tasks that focused on business, business decisions, commercial processes and the factors that lead to personal success or failure.

The Apprentice is a **12-week crash course in business survival** techniques. Grounded in commercial reality, it is not for the faint-hearted. It doesn't claim to turn everyone into an entrepreneur, but if you've got what it takes, you'll recognize yourself and make the best of your natural ability as you read on.

'Anyone who thinks that they can
learn how to be an entrepreneur from
a book will never be an entrepreneur.'

SIR ALAN

What is an apprentice?

Centuries ago, before the days of university degrees, training courses, personal development seminars, MBAs and a host of other routes to acquiring business qualifications, the way to learn a trade was to become an apprentice to a master of the craft. Apprenticeships have their roots in the guilds of the Middle Ages, when tradesmen, craftsmen and students of every discipline would formally undertake to learn their business at the side of a master. Apprentices would earn little, if anything, in the way of wages, and might be expected to pay for their own food and lodgings. Working conditions could be harsh, and they would receive few thanks for their efforts. Their reward, acquired through hard work and learning from the experience of the master, would be skills that would last them a lifetime.

Those who listened well, learnt well, could roll with the punches, worked hard and had the vision to see where success could take them: they had the opportunity to become masters of their craft, leaders in their field and wealthy tradesmen in their own right. Their success would contribute to the economy of the day and enable them to train the next generation. A lot of the most creative and original innovators started off as apprentices: William Morris the craftsman, designer and poet is a prime example. Apprenticeships were a tradition that has continued in professions through history: articled clerks, legal assistants and graduate trainees are modern-day apprentices.

There are now many business leaders who have reinvented the concept of apprenticeships. In both Britain and the USA the value of apprenticeships in business is being increasingly.

What's in it for you?

At heart I am a salesman – a salesman with a creative instinct and a nose for the marketplace. I never put a product into production without knowing what the marketplace wants, what features will make the product attractive to buyers, and what benefits there are to you, the customer, in parting with your hard-earned cash.

I've never been a great believer in business books or self-help books. I am a firm believer that if you've got what it takes, you'll have **a feeling in your gut,** a hunger in your belly – and you'll know you want to be your own boss.

But today's business world is full of challenges, and perhaps it's tougher to make a mark in a world full of high-street brands and big business deals than it was when I was starting out and doing deals along the Tottenham Court Road in London in the early 1970s.

So what's in it for you is **the inside track.** These pages will give you my thoughts **on selling, marketing, self-management, team motivation and how to keep your eye focused on the bottom line.**

It has taken me over 30 years to accumulate my knowledge and experience. I can offer you my own brand of business expertise. It will be short, sharp and from the hip. **If it makes sense to you, then use it. If it doesn't, then don't try and do things my way.** Whatever you do, be true to yourself and find your own style.

I'm not claiming to know it all, and **don't ever call me a business guru because I'm still learning.** It may sound like a cliché, but I learn something new every day.

The knowledge I have comes from the world of selling and manufacturing in electronics. In my field I am a successful businessman, and if my experience can help put an older head on young shoulders, then I am pleased to pass on what I know.

Born to lead or destined to follow?

Why is it that some employees remain technicians or project managers forever while others become innovative leaders, business creators and risk-takers who break the mould, reinvent the marketplace and create their own rules? The truth is, I don't know, but the 12 tasks in *The Apprentice* have been designed to reveal leadership qualities, sales skills, negotiation techniques and team-building ability. This means that these tasks will quickly show up those who haven't got what it takes to succeed in *my* business environment.

Why it is that some people are born to lead and others are better suited to supporting and project-delivery roles is a mystery. There's a need for all sorts in every business – but not in *The Apprentice*.

If you can't stand the heat in this business kitchen, there's only one thing to say…

… 'You're fired!'

ON THE TRAIL OF THE APPRENTICE

PART 1

1
INTRODUCING THE BOARD

Sir Alan Sugar ...

'Probably Britain's greatest entrepreneur.'

RUPERT MURDOCH
Owner of News Corporation Ltd

'He's one of a new breed of British entrepreneurs. I would like to see people like that as role models for young people coming into business. I want people to say, "Damn it, if he can do it, I can!"'

LORD YOUNG
Former Secretary of State for Trade and Industry
talking in the mid 1980s

was very pleased to receive the recognition, quoted on the previous page, from Rupert Murdoch and Lord Young. I had worked hard to build my business, which by the mid 1980s had grown into a multi-million-pound corporation. What I want now is to inspire others – young and not so young – to do the same. I want people to follow their entrepreneurial instincts and become winners in business in their own right. I have been involved in the work of the Prince's Trust and other organizations focused on encouraging the development of personal business skills, especially among young people. I am at a stage in my business and in my life where 'putting something back' is important. *The Apprentice* offered the ideal opportunity to build on this aim, and I hope you enjoy and learn from the result.

I have a reputation for being blunt – a straight talker – and I'm not ashamed of that. Straight talking is honest. It gets to the point. Everyone is clear about what to expect. I don't mean to cause offence, but I won't suffer fools, especially if I have set my sights on a business goal. But I try to combine straight talking with integrity and straight dealing. It's important. Clients, staff and friends know they can trust me, and know that I have the courage of my convictions. I was looking for similar traits in our aspiring Apprentices.

So, is there a secret to being successful? If there were, you can be sure that the company I founded, Amstrad, would have found a way to sell it to the majority of the public by now at a price everyone could afford! However, after 30-odd years in the business I have learnt a thing or two, and it's time to pass that experience on.

Most job applications need a CV – even if you're headhunted, and even if you are the chairman of a company. There is always someone out there who wants to know who you are, what you're made of and what you're worth before they will consider doing business with you. I haven't applied for a job since I was a teenager, but my CV still opens doors and attracts business. Good CVs attract investors, help to build partnerships and tell people, loud and clear, who you are.

For the aspiring business person at a personal crossroads, a CV is also a way of taking stock and refocusing on who you are and where you're at. It's an audit of your achievements, skills and abilities.

I'm including some details from my own CV here, so that you can understand my business path and have a context for what you'll be reading later in the book.

Sir Alan Michael Sugar

Born: 24 March 1947
Married: 1968 Ann Simons; two sons, one daughter, five grandsons

Achievements

- Main shareholder, chairman and Chief Executive of AMSTRAD
- Owner of Viglen
- 13 per cent shareholder of Tottenham Hotspur Football Club
- Owner of AMSHOLD (property and investment company)
- Owner of AMSAIR (executive jet aircraft for chartering)
- 45th on *The Times* Rich List (2004)

Chairman, Amstrad plc since foundation in 1968

Amstrad plc celebrated its thirty-fifth anniversary in 2003. The company (**A**lan **M**ichael **S**ugar **TRAD**ing) started as a small business enterprise and grew rapidly to become an international consumer electronics, telecoms and computer group with wholly owned subsidiaries in France, Germany, Benelux and Denmark, and a worldwide presence through a network of distributors. Stop anyone in the street and they will know the Amstrad name. This high level of brand awareness against giants such as Philips, Sony and IBM was achieved in a relatively short time. Amstrad was responsible for the phenomenal growth in the European personal computer market in the latter half of the 1980s, and was more recently the pioneer of the Europe-wide satellite receiving market.

A mobile telephone company, Dancall Telecom, purchased by Amstrad in 1994 for £6.4 million, was sold to Robert Bosch for £95 million in 1997. Viglen Technology, a computer manufacturing company now known as

Learning Technology, was floated separately on the London Stock Market in 1997, returning some £200 million to Amstrad shareholders. In 2003 that company was, effectively, purchased by my holding company and now operates as a private company based in the UK, and overseas through a subsidiary based in Hong Kong.

Amstrad, of which I hold nearly 30 per cent, is currently launching a series of high-technology, mass-market products onto the UK market.

Chairman, Viglen

I am chairman and majority shareholder in Viglen, one of Britain's largest manufacturers of personal computers. Established over 30 years ago, this company now focuses on the primary and secondary educational markets; it already supplies two-thirds of British universities.

With sales of around £100 million a year, the Viglen brand is now a supplier of choice to the broad educational sector.

Chairman, Tottenham Hotspur plc since 1991

I became chairman of premier league football club Tottenham Hotspur plc in June 1991, and retained that role until resigning in 2001. I remain the company's largest individual shareholder, with a 13 per cent stake. Since becoming involved in the national sport, I have made a significant impact as a commentator and, during my time as chairman, a Premier League motivator on the running and future direction of the game as far as broadcasting, youth policy, the Bosman ruling and financial disciplines are concerned.

Amshold Ltd

Amshold Ltd is my main holding company and is made up primarily of property companies that hold all my real estate interests.

Community interests and positions

- Honorary DSc, City University Business School
- Appointed to Council of the Cranfield Institute
- Chairman of the governors, King Solomon High School, Redbridge
- Supporter of Business in the Community
- Founder and driving force behind the Excalibur Scholarship Scheme
- Honorary chairman, Bristol University Enterprise Centre

Responding to the call from Prime Minister John Major in 1993 to establish a new scheme for graduates from the old Eastern Bloc to study in Britain, I founded the Excalibur Scholarship Scheme. We recruited 21 other leading UK companies as sponsors, thus raising over £1 million. This has enabled more than 20 graduates from Central and Eastern Europe to enrol at British universities each year over the term of the scheme.

As an active supporter of many groups, I frequently address and advise young audiences on business subjects. In recent years I have visited over 20 cities, at the invitation of the chancellor of the exchequer, speaking to young people on the importance of business as a career.

Charitable activities

The Alan Sugar Foundation, established in 1986, has donated millions of pounds to charity, including £1 million for the construction of an old people's home, £600,000 for the construction and upgrading of facilities at the Sinclair House day-centre for old and young in Redbridge, a contribution of £1.3 million to King Solomon High School in Redbridge and nearly £500,000 to the Great Ormond Street Wishing Well appeal. Most recently a donation of £1.3 million was made to rescue the Hackney Empire, which has now been restored. The foundation donates substantial amounts every year to an array of smaller, domestic charities orientated towards welfare. Additionally, I have raised £175,000 (through sponsorship) for the Muscular Dystrophy Group.

Political activities
- Supported and was featured extensively in DTI Single European Market nationwide promotional poster campaign.
- Supported John Major, the then prime minister, with a speech at the pre-election Wembley rally in April 1992.
- Raised £1 million to establish the Excalibur Scholarship Scheme with the prime minister in April 1993.
- Actively supported New Labour in the run-up to the May 1997 election, and have since been recruited by the government to the Treasury's Industry Team, where I am an adviser to Chancellor Gordon Brown on youth enterprise.

People probably know me best as the founder of Amstrad, which started as a small enterprise and has grown to become an international consumer electronics, telecommunications and computer group. I've sold off some of the company, but remain the major shareholder, chief executive and chairman.

So, why did I decide to become CEO for *The Apprentice*? Because I know what it's like to start from scratch without a mentor. **I am a self-made man** with my feet firmly on the ground. I enjoy the benefits of becoming an entrepreneurial success, but at heart I am an old-fashioned entrepreneur. I know my roots and I am proud of them. In spite of some tough times in the press over the years, the public has supported me, and I have both enjoyed success and experienced the challenge of failure through the course of my career.

I can't help the way I am. My East End background might have left me a little **rough around the edges,** but that's not something I can do anything about. It was a good training for reality; it kept me **down to earth** and taught me to quickly appraise situations and assess propositions.

I fought my way out of poverty and I remain convinced that others can do likewise too. Society has been good to me. Now the boot is on the other foot and it's my turn to give something back.

I'd now like to introduce you to the other members of the Board – the people who helped me to assess the candidates in *The Apprentice*, Nick Hewer and Margaret Mountford.

Nick Hewer

Nick is one of my most trusted colleagues. Born to Anglo-Irish parents in England, he was educated by Jesuit priests at Clongowes Wood College in County Kildare, made famous by James Joyce in *A Portrait of the Artist as a Young Man*. After a brief stint as a law student, he diverted to the then novel world of public relations.

Over the next 35 years his work took him all over the world as his consultancy acted for such organizations as Amoco, Securicor, Ciga Hotels, Cable & Wireless, Konica and Tottenham Hotspur. He was retained by the Chantilly-based secretariat of His Highness the Aga Khan in France for over 20 years.

In 1983 he was retained to represent Amstrad, and for the next 21 years became an integral part of the company's management, as well as representing me in my many personal and business interests. Responsible for the company's product launches across Europe and North America, Nick set up and coordinated a network of agencies to handle Amstrad's public relations on a worldwide basis. He was deeply involved in my takeover and chairmanship at Tottenham Hotspur, with its attendant court and newspaper battles. In more recent times he has worked with me on my enterprise initiatives with the government. He now lives in France and spends much time travelling: a lifelong passion.

Nick Hewer knows that once I get behind a project, I'll give it 200 per cent. Having been with me since the beginning, Nick knows me very well, and I value him as a sounding board. He is involved mainly in public relations and promotions, but he's been around whenever we've been buying and selling companies. He's a right-hand man when there's a need to discuss the presentation of business figures to the financial community, the need to organize product launches and generally to interface with the media. He's found me a difficult client because I don't like talking to journalists and I don't particularly like giving interviews, but he always persuades me to go along with him in these matters.

Margaret Mountford

Margaret is a lawyer who specializes in corporate law and has an excellent reputation in the City. She was a partner in the top-tier company Herbert Smith until 1999, and has helped me to win a lot of deals over the past 20 years. She's a fiery character and is the kind of person I like to do business with. She has an excellent way of focusing and getting down to the bottom line. She understands that I need to know certain facts, and she's good at categorizing them, then letting me know what they are.

I trust Nick and Margaret's judgement. It's all very well assessing people face to face, but there were practical tasks being set for the Apprentices and I needed to have eyes and ears that I trusted watching the candidates every step of the way and reporting back to me.

Ideally, I would have loved to have been a fly on the wall 24 hours a day, but that wasn't possible due to my day-to-day commitments. Margaret and Nick have rock-solid integrity – I knew they wouldn't mislead me. If I asked them who did a good job when I was out, I was confident of getting an honest and balanced answer.

'An entrepreneur – if there is such a thing –
is a born schemer who constantly thinks up
new ideas in an original and creative way.'

SIR ALAN

What is an entrepreneur?

What are the main characteristics of an entrepreneur? Are they different from those of a business leader or an effective manager? Of course they are, and I doubt they are skills that can be taught.

Speak to any successful entrepreneur and you will find that few of them had others in their family who shared their drive and hunger to achieve a personal commercial vision, even if they had wholehearted family backing and support. Small businesses are the backbone of the economy in the UK, and the biggest businesses aren't necessarily the most entrepreneurial.

I'm often asked questions that imply there must be some untold secret about how to become an entrepreneur. They are not questions I like answering because **we are all individuals** and I don't believe in formulas for success.

Let me see off some of the more common questions before we begin.

Are entrepreneurs and business leaders born or made?

In my view, **entrepreneurs are born,** but effective business leaders can be made if they are coached well, learn from their mistakes and have the ambition to succeed. However, those who have stayed in the same job all their lives and have reached the age of 40 without doing a deal of some sort, without following an earlier entrepreneurial instinct, are unlikely to suddenly develop entrepreneurial acumen when they hit their mid-life crisis. But who knows? If this sounds like you, and you've got the desire to try, all things are possible – just go for it.

All the Apprentices had experience of running their own businesses with greater or lesser success. Aged between 25 and 39, they included an events manager, an estate agent, a politician, an account director, a business analyst, a headhunter, a restaurateur and some very effective sales and communications experts. They brought with them a range of skills and experience.

How important are training and education?

Training and education are very important. Education trains the brain – certificates prove that you can think – and training can provide some very important skills, but … theory is no substitute for practice and, as anyone who spends even the briefest time with me will testify, I do not rate an MBA above high-street experience in business. If you want to learn, if you want training, get out there and do it in the good old school of hard knocks. **While you're sitting at home reading a book, the next generation of entrepreneurs will be out there hustling.**

The Apprentices were a very mixed bag academically, although each of them was bright and intelligent. Some were graduates, others had left school as soon as they could. A few had professional qualifications, and some had been to business school. I was interested to see which kind of background would provide the most effective survival skills.

Is gender an important factor in becoming successful?

Gender is important in every area of life, but this question usually means how do I rate women as leaders. I'm a great believer and supporter of women in business. Whether someone is male or female means absolutely nothing to me in a business context. Women have been at the helm of some of my most successful business ventures, and Margaret Mountford, a board member on *The Apprentice*, is one of the most formidable legal players in the commercial scene in London.

The woman at the head of my Hong Kong manufacturing business for many years was so good that she ran rings around most people in the UK. Another female employee, a formidable woman, became CEO of Amstrad France. And I also had a woman running the consumer-electronic side of our business in Italy.

In this day and age **there is no distinction between the skills of the sexes.** An old-fashioned person would possibly expect our engineers to be men – probably dressed in bibs and braces. However, engineers today are as likely to be women – and very talented ones too. The qualities that are needed to become a successful and original entrepreneur have nothing to do with gender and everything to do with hard work and organization – skills that are common to both sexes.

There were tough players of both sexes in the teams on *The Apprentice*, and there were many surprises as a result. **Never make assumptions** about gender-specific abilities in business. Nine times out of ten you will be wrong.

Does an entrepreneur need to be a team player?

For an entrepreneur to succeed it is vital that he or she is a team player who can lead from the front while commanding the respect of the team. Entrepreneurs are often mavericks. **A maverick is usually an original thinker** who may be disruptive and difficult to manage. A maverick may also be unpredictable and refuse to be part of the pack. Of course it is easier for entre-preneurs to be true to their own style if they are running the organization rather than trying to fit in as employees, but no one is an island and an entrepreneur is no exception. Adapting from being a one-man band to a team leader or business manager can be one of the hardest leaps that a would-be successful entrepreneur will make. Without the help and support of other people, not only among their own team, but also in partnership with other businesses and business advisers, **a business loner will not survive**.

Operating as part of a team was probably the toughest challenge for our natural leaders because each of them wanted to shine, and many of them had very clear views as to what would and wouldn't work. I was looking out for those who could put their own egos to one side for the good of the team and for the good of the overall goal.

Are risk-taking and courage essential to becoming a successful entrepreneur?

Without doubt, risk-taking and courage are prerequisites to succeeding in business, but **calculated risk** rather than impetuosity or foolhardiness is the thing to aim for. I think of myself as a gambler, but not one driven by addiction. Effective project planning and disciplined time management are essential skills, as is **flexibility of approach** – this last quality probably being the most important attribute of all.

Several of the candidates combined all the necessary skills, so I was looking not just for the best all-rounder, but the one who would fit well into my organization.

So, have you got what it takes?

There are characteristics commonly shared by successful business people and millionaires, so for those who like this sort of thing, I list the recurring attributes opposite.

- Hard work
- Self-belief
- Planning ahead
- Single-minded focus
- Tenacity
- Organizational skills
- Courage
- Decisiveness
- Action-orientated
- Positive thinking
- Being ahead of the game
- Able to visualize success
- Self-discipline
- Proactive approach
- Regular exercise
- Supportive partner or family
- Willing to seek advice from experts
- Learning from, not dwelling on, mistakes
- Gratitude and appreciation
- Faith

Adapted from information in *The Millionaire Mind*, Thomas J. Stanley (Bantam Books, 2000)

Don't think for one minute, however, that just by ticking the right boxes you will automatically have what it takes. I can't stress enough that each of us is an individual with our own indefinable creative flair and unique talents that will ultimately dictate whether we have what it takes to sink or swim in business.

2

INTRODUCING THE CANDIDATES

There could be only one winner on *The Apprentice* but there was no doubt that each of the candidates had what it takes to succeed in business.

'Is there room for more than one
entrepreneur in an organization?'
SIR ALAN

I f a business is hunting for an Apprentice, will it want a creative maverick
and risk-taker who can come up with new ideas, or a safe pair of hands
who can inspire confidence and ensure the company delivers what it has
promised on time and to maximum profit? The ideal would be neither of
those, but a combination of both.

The Apprentice followed the fortunes of 14 dynamic, determined, business-
minded young people, who had the guts to reply to our advert, as they
competed to become the person I want to help me run one of my multi-
million-pound companies. I need to make it clear from the outset that in my
view **this was not a game. It was for real**.

There was no point in bringing together the skills and talents of a group of
people with entrepreneurial spirit, unless they were going to learn something that they could each take away to benefit their own lives.

There may be only one winner in the television series, but each and every
Apprentice has the talent and skill to be a winner in his or her individual
business life.

The candidates for our apprenticeship were:
**Adele • Matthew • Raj • Adenike • Miranda • Saira • Ben
Miriam • Sebastian • James • Paul • Tim • Lindsay • Rachel**

Each of them had unique talents. Some of them I warmed to immediately,
others drove me crazy from the moment they were introduced – but in
business, as in life, it 'takes all sorts', so I put aside my preconceptions and
enjoyed putting them through their business paces.

What was I looking for in the candidates?

The candidates for *The Apprentice* were hand-selected from thousands of applicants. I took as a given that they were bright people with the kind of commercial background that meant they were up for the tasks. I was on the look-out for an intelligent person who could operate alone as well as part of a team and could think independently in an original way. I wanted someone with an **all-round portfolio of skills**, plus strong sales and marketing ability coupled with good organizational abilities.

I did not want someone who expected to learn from a training manual and then implement those lessons. Rather, I was after **someone with innovative ideas** – who was excited about them and had the energy and commitment to take them forward.

Straightforwardness, honesty and integrity are crucial in my company. If you are working with someone who reneges on a deal or who doesn't deliver, things can get tricky. I don't like it when people don't listen, or when they misinterpret what has been said. When you are in business it is important to conduct yourself in a **professional manner** and for people to know they can trust what you say. **Loyalty** is a great thing – a very important quality – but it's hard to judge until you've known people a long time. Only when tricky situations arise and circumstances become confrontational can you start to see whether employees have themselves or the company in mind.

Of vital importance is understanding the **'business buzz'**. If you don't get a buzz from **'doing the deal'**, there is no point in starting a business in the first place. Creating something for your own personal satisfaction is a hobby; sharing the experience with friends and a network of other enthusiasts is also a hobby. It only becomes a business when you start to make hard cash.

'The experience ... showed me that I can be adaptable and flexible. I can turn my hand to almost anything.'

AN APPRENTICE

I needed to know that my chosen Apprentice understood what was meant by a **profit margin** and appreciated the importance of the **bottom line**. I would be seeing that person's character and ability over a long period of time, so I wanted **to pick a jewel** that would sit in the crown of one of my businesses.

Board members Nick Hewer and Margaret Mountford know me and my businesses very well. Although I knew that each decision about the candidates rested ultimately with me, I needed them as my on-screen board members to help me be objective. Each week it was their job to monitor the progress of the two teams of Apprentices and to report back to me on their findings. Their observations were invaluable. After listening to their accounts of proceedings we would give the candidates their opportunity to explain and justify the decisions taken. One team would pass, the other would fail. The failed team would have to face me in the boardroom and one of the members of that team would be fired. A team of 14 Apprentices was eventually whittled down to only two for the final task. It was quite a journey – and tough at times – but we enjoyed every moment of it.

I hoped that one of the Apprentices would have that **entrepreneurial spirit** – that everyone would see it, that it would shine through. It's not something you can hide or camouflage, and it's not something you can pretend to have either. First impressions count, but it is only as you get to know people over time – their working patterns, how they relate to other people, how they rise to a challenge, whether they deliver what they promise – that you get to know their true worth.

If you can guess which of the following candidates ultimately became my Apprentice, I'm impressed. Use the 'Fired or Hired' assessment charts on pages 218 and 220 to make your own assessment.

Adele

- Age 29
- 7 GCSEs; 1 A-level
- Diploma in Performing Arts
- Set up and manages a lucrative property development company
- Currently involved in a five-year project to develop business enterprise software
- General manager of family firm

'Some people call me a workaholic, but I consider I just enjoy work with a passion.'

Adele began her career working in sales at her father's domestic appliance company. Shortly after starting there, she identified several flaws in the business infrastructure and sank her teeth into rectifying the weaknesses and increasing profitability. Nine years and four promotions later, Adele is the company manager and has single-handedly doubled company turnover from £2 million to £4 million.

During her time working in the family business Adele has had to discipline many of her family members and even make some of them redundant: 'It's just business,' she observes.

Employing your own family can be a challenge, but it's something I have done at Amstrad almost since day one. It's important to keep people's pride and integrity intact, but for everyone's sake the business has to remain profitable. Adele will have had some hard decisions to make.

Winning characteristic

Adele is single-minded when it comes to work, and manages to keep her emotions from influencing her business decisions.

She worked until 8 p.m. the night before giving birth, and even managed to sell a kitchen to her midwife while in labour. Now that's recognizing a sales opportunity!

Achilles heel?

Will Adele's direct business style cause conflict among her fellow Apprentices?

You have to recognize and act upon business and sales opportunities in order to succeed. The trick is to maintain a balance, otherwise your relationships with friends and family may suffer as a result.

Adenike

- Age 30
- 9 GCSEs
- BTEC in Business and Finance
- BA in Business Studies
- MA in International Business
- MBA from PACE University, New York
- Owns and manages a top-end restaurant and runs large events for demanding corporate clients

'I am an entrepreneur by nature, and it is all I know.'

Highly educated, with international business experience, Adenike's academic qualifications include an MBA. She is currently the co-owner and managing director of an exclusive cocktail lounge and restaurant in Lagos, Nigeria. True to her entrepreneurial spirit, Adenike literally built the building and business from scratch.

Adenike has a steely nature and is hugely self-confident. Driven from a young age, she always knew she would be a success in business. She describes herself as a self-starter who likes to be hands-on: even though she lives thousands of miles from her restaurant, she is still pivotal in its daily running. I recognize these characteristics as being vital to business success.

Winning characteristic
Adenike has utter self-belief and is a natural leader.

She is quite happy to dominate business situations that she thinks can be improved, and she doesn't take the softly, softly approach. Her determination could take her to the top.

Achilles heel?
Adenike makes herself heard and won't back down, which could ultimately be her downfall.

Adenike hates taking orders, and finds it hard to listen to what other people have to say. But even the most determined business leader needs business partners, and must learn to listen.

Ben

- Age 29
- 1 GCSE
- Certified Senior Account Manager
- Awarded Global Consultant of the Year for the largest executive search company in the world
- Currently running his own headhunting firm

'In my career I win all the time.'

Suave and sophisticated, Ben looks as if he's stepped straight out of the halls of Eton – but in fact he attended his local comprehensive and passed only one GCSE. Oozing with charm and confidence, he cites 'making money' as one of his talents. Money is important to Ben; he sees it as a yardstick to measure his success, and also useful for buying the occasional Cartier watch.

Ben is certainly no fool. At the tender age of 17, with no business experience, he charmed his way into his first job as a trainee search consultant for a leading headhunter. He is already a successful entrepreneur – the founding director of a profitable and dynamic headhunting outfit that produced more than £100,000 of new revenue in its inaugural year. A sharp business sense, self-determination and drive have made Ben the ultimate self-made man. His accomplishments have also been noted by the business community: he has been voted Global Consultant of the Year, beating over 1500 professionals in Europe, the Middle East and Asia by netting over £300,000 worth of business through the creation of a global satellite company.

Winning characteristic
'I'm tenacious, aggressive and forward thinking, with the ultimate gift of the gab.'

Nothing fazes this focused, experienced and highly motivated individual. Ben's confidence shines and his negotiating skills are well honed.

Achilles heel?
After being a sole trader for so many years, will Ben cope when he's not being the boss?

Ben's confidence can sometimes blind him to the opinions of others. He will need to relearn team skills fast.

James

- Age 34
- 9 O-levels; 3 A-levels
- BSc (First Class) in Land Management
- Member of the Royal Institution of Chartered Surveyors (MRICS)
- Securities, Futures and Derivatives Representative (SFDR)
- Finalist in *Property Week*'s Young Property Personality of the Year
- Headhunted to head the UK operation of a private equity real estate fund

'I seek success as a result of my own achievements.'

Highly successful within many large financial institutions, James is the ultimate corporate success story. His huge enthusiasm and engaging charm make it easier to imagine this former public school boy buying sweets from the tuck shop than investing billions of pounds on the stock exchange, but James is in fact a highly respected figure within the investment industry and is quite a mover and shaker in the City of London.

James has followed a textbook career path in finance. His previous employers include two major investment banks, and he is a principal of a pan-European investment fund worth $630 million.

His work experience has taught him how to develop effective business contacts and a personal approach while remaining professional at all times.

In his spare time James enjoys the finer things in life – holidays, all the latest gadgets and Aston Martins!

Winning characteristic
Extremely articulate and commercially astute, James has excellent people skills and the ability to deliver criticism without offending his colleagues.

The trick? He has developed the skill of making people feel good. He is never without a smile on his face and it's impossible to stay angry with James for long.

Achilles heel?
Will James's privileged past be a benefit or a hindrance in the marketplace?

It will be interesting to see whether James can adapt his corporate style to the needs of the tasks and whether he has the steel to fight for the winning position.

Lindsay

- Age 35
- BA in Creative Arts
- Post Graduate Diploma in
  Broadcast Journalism
- Post Graduate Diploma in Internal Communications
  Management
- Founder of the UK's first national car-sharing agency
- Finalist for Cosmopolitan Women of Achievement Awards
- Internal Communications Manager for an oil company

'You must be honest about where you're aiming to go and how you are contracting with others to get there.'

Quietly confident Lindsay exudes calmness and credibility. This successful communications manager is driven and ambitious, but feels no need to shout it from the rooftops. Her down-to-earth manner has served her well as she climbs the ranks within an international oil company. Alongside her skills as a natural mediator and team player, Lindsay has strong moral values, which make her firm and fair at work. She likes to ensure that everyone has a say, and she's not afraid to stand up to authority.

While in her twenties, Lindsay started two lucrative businesses that brought her nationwide acclaim. The first was a comedy café, run more as a labour of love than a business. The second was a true entrepreneurial success: the UK's first national lift-sharing agency. This operated for four years and at the height of trading had 17,000 members.

Winning characteristic
Calm and self-assured, Lindsay will slowly but surely make her mark.

She is well organized, a thorough planner with no shortage of ideas, and has the talent to shine.

Achilles heel?
Have Lindsay's corporate skills dulled her entrepreneurial edge?

She will need to be flexible and quick thinking when there is a variety of options on the table.

Matthew

- Age 39
- BA in Business and Computing
- Post Graduate Diploma in Marketing
- Member of the Institute of Marketing
- Self-qualified stockbroker regulated by the Securities and Futures Authority
- Conservative parliamentary candidate

'The object of a business is not to make money. The object of a business is to satisfy customers. The result is to make money.'

Matthew is the oldest Apprentice – a recent business-school graduate and self-styled entrepreneur. He possesses a rich and diverse work history.

He began his career with the Conservative Party, then worked variously for a London branch of the Chamber of Commerce and a Moscow-based direct marketing firm. After qualifying as an authorized financial adviser, he saw the opportunity to go solo, and started his own company offering financial advice over the Internet.

Three years ago he returned to his political roots, and stood for election to Parliament as a Conservative Party candidate. He failed to win the seat, so instead dedicated himself to further study, recently completing a BA in business and computing.

Winning characteristic
Matthew's boundless enthusiasm and willingness to get involved cannot be faulted, especially during the business tasks.

He has no shortage of ideas, and he has the tenacity to ensure they get heard.

Achilles heel?
Matthew isn't wrong when he says his worst quality is a lack of diplomacy.

I know what it is like to be accused of having an 'attitude problem', and it may prove to be a challenge for Matthew. His manner is not to everyone's liking.

Miranda

- Age 26
- 8 GCSEs
- BTEC National Diploma
  in Performing Arts
- GNVQ in Leisure and Tourism
- Owned a successful mail-order directory company for
  performing arts professionals
- Founder of her own market and exhibitions display company
- Managing director of a commission-based estate agency

'I've got huge life experience for my age, which is better than anything written on a piece of paper.'

Miranda has already launched two successful companies and is currently set-ting up her third – a commission-based, American estate-agency franchise. She landed her first sales job aged 12, and has been working ever since. Now 26, Miranda is the youngest and most image-conscious of our Apprentices.

In the past, Miranda has been a very lucrative employee – one of Britain's highest-earning 'Hooter' girls in the restaurant chain of the same name, starting out as a waitress and quickly climbing the ranks of management. Her ex-boss obviously appreciated her, saying that 'her sales technique and the profits she generated for the company remain legendary.'

Miranda has some of the drive that I had when I was first starting out. She has turned her personal sales experience into profit for her own enterprises.

Winning characteristic

'I create eye contact, introduce a little "audience participation" to generate laughter and it's at this point that the customer forgets you're trying to sell them something and lets their guard down, leaving me free to enter their subconscious craving to buy my product!'

With a well-honed understanding of human nature, Miranda can manipulate her customers to the point where they're begging her for the product.

Achilles heel?

Is Miranda all preparation and presentation, or is she a woman of substance?

Enthusiasm and showmanship have taken Miranda a long way; it will be interesting to see how these qualities work in more hard-nosed settings.

Miriam

- Age 26
- 4 A-levels
- BA in French and Spanish
- Manager of an exclusive hotel in the French West Indies
- Founder of an events management company

'I don't know all the classic business theories or have the "pat" answers – my experience comes from what I've directly learnt in the field.'

Miriam was working and residing on the exclusive island of St Martin in the French West Indies when she was selected as a finalist for *The Apprentice*. Two years previously she had spotted a niche opportunity on the island and seized the chance to set up an events management company to provide a high-quality events planning service 'where excellence comes as standard'. But this was not enough to satisfy high-flying Miriam – she is also the general manager of an exclusive hotel, where she has had 'nothing but praise from my clients'.

Astonishingly, Miriam made a 20-hour round trip to attend each stage of the interview process. When questioned why she took the chance of spending a considerable amount of cash on the air fares, 26-year-old Miriam coolly replied, 'It's an investment for the future'.

Winning characteristic
'I have originality of approach and method because I don't come from a business-school background. I bring a unique perspective as I've lived in four different countries and am multi-lingual.'

Miriam has the organization skills, motivation and drive to succeed.

Achilles heel?

Miriam's businesses are focused on providing excellent service to her clients. Will she remember that safeguarding the bottom line is more important than high-quality delivery in The Apprentice*?*

The tasks will show whether she can lead from the front and command the respect of her team members.

Paul

- Age 34
- 9 O-levels
- Basic and advanced sales for an international car dealership
- Work and Method Study Certificate
- Systems Analysis Certificate
- Founder of a lucrative property management company

'I know I'm not the cleverest bloke in business, so I always make sure I check everything, and then I check and check again. That's why I'm a success, because that's what other people don't do. That's how I'll win this show.'

A born salesman, Paul admits he's not very academic, but his energy and charm more than make up for it. As a self-made man, he is very proud of his meteoric rise in the business world. He has made his way through his own efforts and is the sole owner of a property rental and development empire.

Having left school with unremarkable qualifications, Paul believes that his considerable achievements are a product of his hawk-like attention to detail.

Paul holds traditional values and can find it difficult to take orders from a woman. He is excitable, warm and engaging, but when criticized, displays a very fiery temper.

Winning characteristic
Paul is a passionate perfectionist who is not afraid of hard work and who has the determination and ambition to go to the top.

I recognize a lot of my younger self in Paul, he is hungry for success and I can see his strengths and abilities.

Achilles heel?
Paul is a man of honesty an integrity, but he has a short fuse and his fiery temper reared its head quite early on.

He has a strong character. Will he be able to manage his emotions effectively? Self-discipline is crucial for success at senior level in business.

Rachel

- Age 32
- 4 A-levels
- BA in German
- Chartered Institute of Management Advanced Certificate
- Fund-raising manager for one of the largest national children's charities

'I have incredible presence and am one of those people who fills a room even when alone. I have an infectious desire to live life to the full.'

Rachel brings over 10 years' postgraduate work experience to the table. Her previous roles include being an advertising sales executive, a conference developer, a sales and marketing manager and an account director. Rachel is a very socially-minded woman, who is determined to play a fair game, and would rather eat her own arm than stab a fellow human being in the back.

Full of fun and always ready for a laugh, eccentric Rachel has few inhibitions and is willing to try anything once! Will her consensual business style translate from charity fund-raising to the corporate world?

Winning characteristic
Rachel believes that in business you should keep your promises and behave towards others as you would like them to behave towards you.

Rachel has a creative and highly inclusive approach. Her moral fibre and her ability to get on with anyone make her a valuable player who has plenty of experience in 'making things happen'.

Achilles heel?
Could Rachel's desire to be liked prove greater than her desire to succeed?

There are some strong characters among the Apprentices, and there are those who could try to take advantage of Rachel's personable management style. Will they or she come unstuck?

Raj

- Age 30
- 8 GCSEs; 3 A-levels
- LLB in Law (upper second)
- Founder and managing director of an estate agency

'I'm an entrepreneur, not an angel!'

Raj is extremely confident in his business abilities. He has grit and determination, and is a true all-rounder.

Self-employment was always the ideal way forward for ambitious maverick Raj: 'I get bored and frustrated if I can't get my own way, so it's better for me to work for myself.' His first solo business venture was a new concept in estate agency that utilized freelance staff at all stages of the selling process. Within 18 months profits were soaring and Raj expanded the business, increasing the number of employees from two to 40. However, he failed to get the £1.5 million in venture capital required to keep the business afloat, so was declared personally bankrupt. This setback has not dented Raj's self-belief, and he will definitely make a successful comeback.

I don't hold his bankruptcy against him. Winning the confidence of the City can be a major challenge, and you need good advice to learn how it operates. Raj has many entrepreneurial characteristics. It will be interesting to see how he performs in the group.

Winning characteristic
Self-belief, self-confidence and great technical skills.

Raj is completely single-minded, and his all-round skills will be an asset to any team.

Achilles heel?
'I'll do the best I can and that'll be good enough.'

Is Raj's self-confidence well founded? His best will need to be at least 100 per cent to succeed as an entrepreneur. He will need to demonstrate how hungry he is for success to make it through this 12-week job interview.

Saira

- Age 34
- 4 O-levels; 2 A-levels
- BA in Humanities
- MA in Environmental Planning
- Corporate sales manager for an online recruitment company

'I hope that as an Asian woman I will give other Asian women the inspiration to go out there and do well in business.'

Saira is a sales manager with an enormously powerful sense of self-belief backed by a strong work ethic. Highly emotional and ambitious, Saira believes she was born to be a leader and believes the adage that you should always 'be true to yourself'.

She started her working life as a town planner, but opted for a change of direction at the age of 28, when her sales and marketing career took off. Since then she has excelled in a variety of roles and now earns a significant sum per annum selling online recruitment packages to FTSE 300 companies.

A chronic over-achiever, her drive extends to her leisure time. She is a fully qualified fitness instructor and a self-confessed gym freak. She also speaks four languages other than English – Urdu, Bhari, Punjabi and Hindi.

Saira's belief is that if you want something badly enough you can make it happen. She even delayed her wedding plans when she was selected to take part in *The Apprentice*, recognizing that it was a once-in-a-lifetime opportunity.

Winning characteristic
Saira's self-belief is unshakeable.

Her dedication to hard work, combined with her ambition and her sales ability, will make her a determined contestant.

Achilles heel?
Saira is not afraid to speak her mind.

Her style may grate on some members of the group, who may feel they are being bulldozed, so it will be interesting to see how she performs as part of a team and whether she stays the course.

Sebastian

- Age 29
- 4 A-levels
- BSc in Natural Science
- Securities Institute Diploma
- Registered member of the Financial Services Authority
- MBA from INSEAD
- Commercial pilot's licence

'I have no doubt that I am a superb candidate for *The Apprentice.'*

Dressed in his Savile Row suits, Sebastian is the epitome of a classically handsome gent. He skis, glides, plays a mean game of tennis and is a certified commercial pilot who enjoys 'doing acrobatics in powerful planes'. If Sebastian had a famous counterpart, it would probably be James Bond. He has just completed his MBA and is living in Paris.

Kicking off his career as an analyst in the cut-throat world of investment banking in London, Sebastian moved into corporate finance and has acted in an advisory capacity to worldwide corporations in Chile, Argentina and London. He likes to play with the big boys: one of his most significant achievements to date is executing over $3 billion worth of cross-border (collateralized), tax-effective fund-raising and investment transactions.

Winning characteristic
Highly intelligent and articulate, Sebastian also has daredevil courage and understands how business works.

He has a creative business brain and his personal qualities should stand him in good stead when the going gets tough.

Achilles heel?

Sebastian sometimes comes across as being 'to the manor born', with a strong belief in the power of his qualifications.

Has he got what it takes to sell for survival? Can he get 'down and dirty' to chase the bottom line, or will his reliance on business theory slow him down?

Tim

- Age 27
- 11 GCSEs; 3 A-levels
- BSc in Psychology
- Chartered Institute of Personnel and Development Diploma

'Sir Alan has a lot he could teach me, and perhaps I might know a few things that I could teach him as well.'

After graduating in psychology from Middlesex University, Tim joined the graduate trainee programme within a public sector organization and is now a specialist in management information. He has been responsible for delivering projects valued up to £5 million.

Tim's background echoes my own in some respects, as he grew up in the East End of London. Brought up in a single-parent family 'watching my mum work her fingers to the bone' strengthened Tim's will to succeed. His self-confidence belies his youth. He's walked the rocky road from the streets of East Ham to the boardroom, and there is no doubt that high-octane Tim will use his 'maximum energy' to fight his way to the top of the tree.

Winning characteristic
'I have a young approach, together with a good old-fashioned-hard-work ethic.'

Charismatic and sharp, Tim watches everything and misses nothing. He is seen as everybody's friend, and sees being a team player as crucially important in the workplace.

Achilles heel?

Tim is short on commercial experience and has a lot to learn. Has he got what it takes to be a success in business?

Tim will need to prove himself to be a fast learner and able to develop business acumen if he is to go all the way to the top.

3

HOW TO BE AN APPRENTICE

apprentice – **a person who is learning an art or trade either from an employer to whom he or she is bound by a contract or by practical experience under skilled workers.**

DICTIONARY DEFINITION

recognised elements of my younger self in each of the candidates who joined me on *The Apprentice*. They were all hungry young people who had already had some experience of running their own show. I was interested to know whether they had the ability to think like winners, whether they had the stamina to succeed, who could 'lead from the front' and who was more likely to 'hide in the bushes' rather than push themselves forward; whether they were able to enjoy what they did at work whilst maintaining a balance in their leisure hours, and whether they had a proactive vision of the future.

How hungry are you?

When I first started out, I wasn't interested in making a million, I wasn't thinking about getting a knighthood. It was about getting some wheels. I wanted a car – and I wanted to be independent. I was also angry, and probably a bit arrogant. I was sick of putting money in other people's pockets when I knew I could earn more on my own. I had seen my father work hard all his life, putting the family first and playing the safe game in order to take care of us. I was at a point when I had no responsibilities – and I knew I didn't have his temperament – I would never be able to stay the course working for someone else. It wasn't a conscious wish to do things differently, but the more I worked for other people, the more I knew I'd rather go it alone.

That was the starting point, and it wasn't an empty, impulsive action. I had money saved up, and in spite of taking what some thought was a foolhardy step, I took it with care. I withdrew £100 of my savings, of which £50 went on wheels (distribution), £8 went on third-party insurance (liability), and the balance of £42 went on stock (investment). I already knew my market

'The benefit of coming from a poor background and a loving family is that the only way is up.'

AN APPRENTICE

(market research) and I knew the main players (purchasing and sales). I had a personal target of £60 per week (business planning), which I aimed to earn by the Wednesday of each week (self-discipline and application). I worked hard to create a place for myself as an effective middleman and deal-maker (negotiation).

It was only after I had been doing my own thing for a while and had the satisfaction of knowing I was making a success of it, that I began to think seriously about exploiting new opportunities – of speculating with new product development. That company, launched in 1967, rose to be valued at £1.2 billion in the mid 1980s.

Overnight success? There's no such thing. Hard graft, self-discipline and the hunger to succeed are the keys.

Personal vision
Clarify your goal
Having a **vision** is about using your imagination, it is about stretching your brain to think differently. It's about training yourself to **focus** on where it is you want to go, what it is you want to achieve.

A vision is important because if you can't see yourself living your life differently, if you can't envisage a world where your product, your service, your idea is necessary for others' business success, then you don't know where you are headed. It would be like going on holiday without a destination and no road map. You will get somewhere – anywhere – and you might enjoy the view, but you don't know where you are, so you can never tell others how to find the location, and you can never go back there.

Having **goals** is vital because they are the stepping-stones to achieving your vision. Without goals your vision remains a dream. That's obvious, you might say, but it is amazing how many businesses fail because they don't know where they are in the marketplace; they haven't got a business plan and they are not monitoring their progress.

All sorts of statistics declare that a large percentage of businesses fail within the first 1–3 years of starting up. It is hard to be accurate about this, but look at these examples: in 2002 some 91 per cent of businesses registered for VAT in that year were still in business 12 months later; 64 per cent of those registered for VAT in 1998 were still in business three years later. It's an easy thing to write down, but a harder thing to live through. These figures mean that at least 36 per cent of those people who started up in 1998 did not succeed in the longer term. Their vision and goals were not focused enough to help them survive.

There was a high level of self-belief and self-motivation amongst the Apprentices. I was confident that each of these young people had the energy and wisdom to succeed in business.

Take action

- If you are thinking about setting up your own business, choose something that you love and have experience in. Map it out: find out what you know, and ask others about the things you don't know.
- Don't worry about making mistakes because it is from mistakes that most people learn.
- Be bold. Set a target date and a series of goals.
- If you're thinking about it, do it! There are no free lunches out there. You can only achieve your ambition by giving it a try.

> 'If you don't believe in what you are
> doing 100 per cent you won't succeed.'
>
> **AN APPRENTICE**

Desire

Understand what or who inspires you

The **desire to succeed** needs to come **from deep within** – it's not something you can fake. You need to know yourself and be aware of who your role models and mentors are. Who do you admire? Whose success would you like to emulate? You need to realize what you are trying to get away from, as well as what you want to move towards.

Perhaps you've got your vision, mapped out an immaculate business plan and set your goals. Are you raring to go, or are you feeling stuck? Desire is what you need to set you off on the path to becoming an entrepreneur.

The word 'entrepreneur' winds me up because so many people claim to be one, but very few really are. You can't learn to be an entrepreneur. It's something that is in you. You can learn to play the piano and knock out a few nice tunes, but you'll never be a Mozart; you can learn to paint a house and it will look very smart, but you're never going to be a Van Gogh. In the same way, an MBA on its own won't make you a success in business; a business plan won't guarantee motivation or achievement of your goals. The idea on its own is not enough.

What makes you tick? Are you motivated by making money or the idea you are planning to launch?

Two kinds of people run big companies: those who started the business and have a major shareholding, and those who just have a job. Their mindsets are quite different. The first has the business at heart and is permanently focused on it performing as it is meant to. Salary is not a big concern; the real reward is a successful company. The second type, the jobbers, are more interested in what they get out of it. Once established, they tend to look after number one, covering their backsides when anything goes wrong. They care about themselves, but do they truly care about the business? Have they got the desire that would drive them to be successful entrepreneurs in their own right?

It was important to me that my final candidate selected from *The Apprentice* process would have the overall good of my businesses in mind, not to their own detriment, but with a true understanding of 'the business of business'. It is valuable to keep abreast of who's who, and who has achieved what in business and to keep abreast of the business news.

Take action
- Who are your positive role models or mentors? Do you have any?
- What qualities do you admire in others who have achieved their goals?
- What is really pushing you forward at this moment? Is it a positive or negative reason? Both can be motivating, but is it enough to make you really crave success?

Drive
Maintain your own momentum
Anyone who watched the athletics during the Athens Olympics in 2004 would have been struck by the sheer **hunger and focus** of those athletes determined to win against very stiff odds. Nowhere was this more obvious than in the running events. The athletes who won gold medals knew their form and pace. They had trained hard, they had the desire to win, but they also had the **drive to succeed**. They had planned the race; they had studied the form of the competition; they had trained – very, very hard – so they

understood their personal strengths and what they could deliver. That meant knowing when to push and, crucially, knowing when not to push, in order to get ahead. The athletes who tried to accelerate when their bodies were already performing at optimum speed came in second, third or nowhere at all. The ones who had pushed at the right point and stayed focused on maintaining their momentum were the ones who powered over the finish line.

There is great similarity between the mental discipline required to train for sporting success and that needed to make it in business. There is no way that you will consistently beat the rest of the pack without training and without building up your skills. You need to **start small but think big**.

To succeed in business you need drive, energy, determination, hunger – and you also need the **discipline** to stay focused, to build your momentum and to maintain a steady pace. There are those who think that running your own business means an easier life. Far from it. When everyone else is clocking off at 5 p.m. you'll still be working. But you will learn your pace; you will learn that coming to a complete halt makes it far harder to start up again.

Doing a deal is like a sprint, but **building a business** is more like a marathon. And just like a marathon runner, it is better to build gradually and aim to maintain a steady pace than to crash and burn.

There are many enthusiastic, would-be entrepreneurs out there who promise too much, too soon. In the first flush of new business development they make hundreds of calls, they promise the earth to all and sundry, they have such a large range of credit and payment arrangements that the customers have to remind them what the current terms of business are. Planning goes out of the window. Contact is either feast or famine. This stop-start approach does no one any favours. Clients don't know what to expect; they don't know what the business is offering, or whether it is reliable. There's nothing wrong with the level of drive that this person has; the problem is that he or she is not building and maintaining momentum. There's nothing wrong with being flexible – in fact it's essential – but don't let others pull your strings. **Stay proactive** and keep that entrepreneurial start-up energy flourishing.

Sell anything, anywhere. Don't be particular if someone wants to buy – sell to them. **But only make deals that you can deliver on**. Be conscious that you are developing your client base with every call you make. Keep your cool and play to your strengths. **Plan ahead**. Be clear about what you are offering, and keep an open mind for new opportunities.

Set your pace and keep in training. When you're going for gold **there's no room for self-indulgence**. It was hard for some of the Apprentices to see how this applied to them because there were time constraints applied to each task. But, in business, time management is important, so that was not the point. The point was that first impressions count and relationships matter. I would be watching how each candidate conducted him or herself in business.

Take action
- Set personal targets and seek to surpass them.
- Know your working pace. Plan ahead to make maximum use of your day, and to ensure you start focused and maintain momentum.
- Stay focused and avoid developing self-indulgent habits during the working day. A pattern of late starts, long lunches and late-night working all hand the advantage to your competitors.

> 'Stamina and energy are
> crucial to success in business.'
> **AN APPRENTICE**

- Be aware of your time and use it to its optimum.
- Make sure you are in control, even when you feel as if you're not.

Capacity for hard work
Can you deal with adversity?
There are those who **work hard**, and there are those who think they work hard. There are also those who work very, very hard for a very long time, but don't recognize the progress they have made, so they quit, just before the winning post.

Have you got staying power when times are hard? When you think back over your life to date, did success or material goods come easily to you at school, at home, in your social life? When has your endurance been tested, and how did you react? If you're faced with adversity, do you avoid the problem or procrastinate, or – even worse – do you lose your cool or blame others? **Can you keep working when everything seems stacked against you**?

I've never been the wining-and-dining type myself. I think it's a waste of time. If you're the sort of person who thinks a hard day's work starts at 11 a.m. with a cappuccino in a café and finishes at 3 p.m. after a long lunch, then (depending on who you had lunch with, of course) you're unlikely to make it as a successful entrepreneur. You're probably either employed by someone else or have a large private income. Wake up! The 1980s are behind us and the dot.com boom is over. Investors are unlikely to invest in pipedreams any more.

People who have a chance of success in business are those who know what it's like to have their backs against the wall and still come out on top with their integrity intact. They are the ones who have a competitive edge, for whom winning – against all odds – is everything; they listen, dream large and plan with care; they are not afraid to ask questions, are dogged in their determination, and have no qualms about bucking the system. They are not necessarily the high-fliers who get all the plaudits; they are the ones who know what's going on at ground level, the ones who chip their way up the ladder, cannily, steadily, one step at a time. They are the ones who will be determined to solve a problem rather than give up.

Make no mistake – **there is no such thing as luck in business** – just hard graft, and keeping your antennae tuned to changes in the marketplace. There were winers and diners as well as grafters amongst the Apprentices. I wanted to find out what each of them was truly made of when they had a tight deadline and had to knuckle down to the task in hand.

Take action

- Watch your attitude. Do you think you are owed something by your employer, by your family, by society? If so, think again. Get out there and start creating your own opportunities if you want to succeed in your own right.
- Don't give up, no matter how hard you've been trying. If you believe in something, it is worth continuing with it – not blindly and not without taking stock of your progress to date – but if you've asked yourself the tough questions (see pages 79–80) and you believe you have an original and marketable idea, keep going (after taking professional advice, if necessary).
- Don't expect overnight success. You can strike lucky if you have the right product in the marketplace at the right time and at the right price, but true success takes years, and a lot of trial and error.
- You feel like quitting? Keep on trying just one more time …

'Believe in your goal. As long as you
believe in it – you can achieve it.'

AN APPRENTICE

Do you think like a winner?

I come from a working-class family. We lived in a council flat in Hackney, east London. At that time it was generally accepted that when you left school you went straight to the local garment factory. I had earned myself a reputation as someone who could broker a good deal and who had a talent for selling, so I found myself on a slightly different path – in consumer retail goods.

I learnt early on that it paid to **think big** and **think smart**. In my early role as a salesman selling tape recorders, rather than selling my heart out for a single-unit order, it dawned on me that I could earn much more for the same (or possibly less) effort if I targeted the chief buyer at Currys and aimed for larger orders of, say, 1000 units.

I looked for bigger deals and I landed some sizeable orders, but my success at selling was never reflected in my payslip. Instead, my boss penalized me for the special discounts he had to give the larger customers as a result of my order – even though I was increasing his bottom line. I lost my temper and walked out of that job. Something similar happened in my next job: again I saw red and walked out. Those bosses did me a favour. Had they not been so ungrateful, and had I not got mad, I might still be working for one of them today. Instead, they reinforced my belief in myself and made me determine that one day I would work for myself.

To be a successful business entrepreneur, you need more than just a competitive edge. **You need a hide like a rhino**, the ability to operate way outside normal comfort zones, a willingness to reinvent the rules, and total, utter, complete self-belief – against all odds.

> 'Look at what you've achieved in life and
> be confident that you made it possible.'
> **AN APPRENTICE**

Self-belief is a critical skill for success in business. Although they had different ways of expressing it, self-belief was a trait that each of *The Apprentice* candidates shared.

Self-belief

If you don't believe you can, why should anyone else?

Do you believe in yourself? Do you know that you have what it takes to succeed? Or are there seeds of doubt? If you naturally defer to others, apologize for your success or don't really believe you can make it, then it won't matter how much financial backing you have, it won't matter how good your product is and it won't matter how much others believe in you. You are your own number one obstacle, and you need to **change your attitude** – fast!

It may seem an obvious thing to say, but **an entrepreneur needs more backbone** than most. You are trying to develop a new concept, but no one else shares your vision; you are trying to deliver to your customers, but the supplier lets you down at the last minute; you are trying to get stock into your nationwide outlets, and your distributor goes bankrupt; you have set up a press launch for a ground-breaking new product line, and the technology lets you down.

When you're running your own show, **the buck stops with you** – no one else. You are the product, you are the service, you are the reason for failure. It gets up close and personal. And that can hurt – if you take it personally. This was a lesson that some of the Apprentices found quite hard.

In reality, **we all learn from our mistakes** – and our failures. The fact is that you cannot succeed if you don't try, and you can't learn without making mistakes. The larger the failure, the bigger the lesson, and the closer you are to success next time. Perfectionism can be a big barrier to progress because it can provoke feelings of failure and hopelessness. Much better to look at what you got right, and to adjust the rest.

Entrepreneurs often have a reputation for being difficult, for ignoring the reasons why not, and listening only to the 'can do' response. That's because a true entrepreneur will aim to overcome all odds. Look at James Dyson. He's been quoted as saying that success is made up of 99 per cent failure. The ones who succeed are the ones who say, 'OK, I'll give it another go. I don't care what anyone thinks'. Perhaps we'd still be living by gaslight if Edison or Swan had given up at the first sign of 'failure' when they were designing their prototypes for the light bulb!

There is a sales-training truism that it can take on average 20 people saying no before you get to a yes. Why are sales people so often upbeat and positive? Because they welcome the nos if it means they are getting closer to the yes. The trick is to try and **convert the initial no into a yes** – and fast, so that you cover more ground. And that needs a fast brain, guts and determination.

I'm not saying you shouldn't listen to feedback from your own business advisors and colleagues – especially if you respect the view of the person who is delivering it – but be your own person.

No one else is living your vision, no one else has your drive, no one else knows what is going through your mind – and **no one else knows what you are made of**.

Unless the person who is offering the advice has enjoyed years of success and is basing that advice on knowledge and experience, have the guts to trust your instincts – provided you've put your basic business building blocks in place (see pages 138–39).

Take action

- Watch your response to failure. If you are taking setbacks personally, or taking failure out on others, or drinking, smoking or eating too much as a way of coping, give yourself a talking to and re-focus on your goal. Take stock of the business plan and review what's going on in the marketplace. When you've figured out what you've been doing wrong, adjust it and try again.
- Take action, don't take refuge in self-pity. If you start feeling sorry for yourself, your competitors will gain the advantage without doing a thing.
- Modesty may be an admirable quality, but not when it comes to business. If you're selling your services or promoting a product, your clients want to be able to believe in what you're offering them. Make sure you come across as a safe bet.
- If you have a problem with confidence, hide your fear. Feeling nervous and uncertain in new situations is normal. You'll soon adapt.

The will to win

Do you have the desire to succeed?

There's no doubt that if you don't care about winning, you probably won't win – not in the long run anyway. To succeed you need a **competitive edge**.

In many ways my approach to business is similar to my approach to sport. I play tennis. I will never be a brilliant player, but I can serve a good match.

'Teamwork is critical to success.
United we win, divided we fall.'

AN APPRENTICE

I enjoy it because it combines keeping fit with exercising the mind. It is fast, fun and strategic.

When I first began playing tennis I would deliberately choose to play people who were better than me. **I wanted to challenge myself** to win, to learn, to become the best I could be as fast as I could. Now that I can play reasonably well I also enjoy competing against people who are the same level, or perhaps not as good as me, because it allows me to hone my game, to **practise my skills** in a controlled way.

Tennis offers interesting parallels with my business experiences. As the new kid on the block, I had to prove myself, and move fast to cope with the might and weight of the big-boy retailers on the high street. Now, as I no longer have to prove myself, my company can take time when developing a new product, testing it against what we know from past experience and, while still putting ourselves ahead of the game, we no longer need to take such a high-risk strategy in order to improve.

Our candidates were each taking part in *The Apprentice* to win – and they each wanted and had the will to win. The greatest challenge was learning how to balance the needs of the team with their own goals and desires – but they eventually learned that **the individual cannot succeed alone**. The combined talents and success of the team is crucial to overall and continued success.

Take action
* How much do you care about winning? Do you keep challenging yourself to learn better techniques? Make sure you are not being complacent. To succeed you need to stay ahead of the game.

- Which is more important to you, personal recognition or the bottom line? Providing excellent service or making a profit? It is admirable to want to help others and understandable that you would like to be noticed, but unless you're running a service industry, gaining plaudits won't pay the bills.
- Visualize what it is like to win – and enjoy the feeling. Winning comes with its own pressures and responsibilities. If being a winner is outside your personal comfort zone, you'll be better off remaining someone else's employee.

Originality and creativity
Staying ahead of the 'me toos'

In my business **it is crucial to be original**, to stay ahead of the rest of the market-place. If you're manufacturing a mass-market electronic product, i.e. producing the cheapest product with the most features, which will be attractive to most people, you are competing mainly on margin. In spite of your original features, you can be sure that eventually someone will find a way to copy it.

Apparently, copying is the highest form of flattery. I don't know about that, but I call the result a 'me too' product. 'Me too' products are created by companies that don't have the imagination to break new ground, or that have a 'safety first' policy, following rather than leading the marketplace. Once the 'me toos' start selling my products, I start thinking about what comes next.

Complacency is the death-knell of a company because the market is always changing, trends are always changing, and your competitors are always changing. Never be complacent. Just because something sold well last week doesn't mean that it will next week. If the 'me toos' are on to my idea, then the market is on the move.

> 'Being adaptable is
> critical in business.'
> **AN APPRENTICE**

Experience of a market is invaluable because you start to understand what sells and what doesn't, and you can begin to assess more easily what will work and what won't – but with that comes another danger: making assumptions.

Never make assumptions – even about something you think you already know. Always ask the marketplace, always test your product, always make sure that your margin is enough to make a profit and that you're selling to a niche that can afford to buy at your price.

Several of the tasks set for the Apprentices included elements of creativity and originality. I wanted to see how the candidates thought, how market savvy they were and whether they had the nous to ask available experts for help and advice. Few of them had worked in a creative environment before and it was an area fraught with challenges.

In my companies I am the creative hub. I generate the majority of new ideas. This is both a strength and a weakness. It is a strength because the City and the markets have learnt to trust that there is an awful lot we do right; it is a weakness because if I were to disappear tomorrow, the creative future of the company would be at risk. It is something I am very conscious of and that we're looking to address right now. That's why, in a mature company, choosing the new generation of staff is so important.

Take action
- Are you an original thinker or do you build on or copy other people's ideas? Start testing your ideas on those you trust or on the marketplace – will they fly?
- Do you imagine the future as a place that is more exciting and

innovative than it is now? You've got the right attitude. Are you nostalgic for the past? Use your nostalgia to find ideas that will work in the present, otherwise you may not have the flexibility to survive in the modern world.

- Don't feel threatened by the competition. Stay awake to what is going on in the marketplace, but don't panic and start copying when you get cold feet. Stay ahead of the pack.
- Never forget that the customer is always right. This means making sure you can sell your ideas well enough that they are not questioned, and being willing to listen to what people say. Sometimes innovators and entrepreneurs are so far ahead that others need time to catch up.

Imagination and thinking big
Visualize living the dream
People ask me whether I started out with a vision of being a multi-millionaire. But that is the wrong question. What's so important about becoming a multi-millionaire?

There are many thousands of successful entrepreneurs and business people who will never be multi-millionaires. Does that mean they are not successful? Does that mean they are not thinking big? Far from it. They are the backbone of the economy and each one is a success in their own right. If all you are looking for is lifestyle, you need to head for a business sector that pays well or make sure your inherit some wealth. There are no personal guarantees via the entrepreneurial route.

My interpretation of **thinking big** is rooted in business and sales. Thinking big means **thinking strategically** and planning **the optimum deal**. The optimum deal is not necessarily the largest or biggest, and is unlikely to be the lowest risk. Thinking big means looking to shift your product, or to supply your service to the biggest marketplace possible. That's where creativity and imagination come in, because you need to look constantly at how to reach your market in a new way. For example, cable television is making increasing use of US-style shopping channels – as our Apprentices found out.

Make sure you know who the big players are in your market sector and that you have a reason why they should want to do business with you.

My imagination and creativity remain focused on the marketplace – what it wants, what it needs and how we might deliver it. Get that right and the rest will follow.

Anyone who knows me or has read my newspaper columns over the years will know I have very little patience with profit and deals made out of thin air (perhaps that should be hot air). During the dot.com boom of the 1990s, millions of dollars were made and lost on the stock exchange on the back of great ideas that weren't founded on substance. These were people and companies that were thinking big all right, but at what long-term cost to themselves and the economy? I'm a great believer in building success on solid foundations that will last – and that will serve your family, your community and, by implication, your country and future generations.

Imagination and visualization are important because you need to believe you can succeed – but make sure your feet are on the business ground because, to my knowledge, Walter Mitty (the fictional character who lived in a fantasy world) never made it big.

Take action

- Be ambitious and keep your dreams real. Rein in the impulse to act on your lifestyle fantasies until you have the right financial foundation stones in place.
- Remember that all success starts in selling the right product or service to the marketplace. If you don't know what your market wants, don't guess – ask.
- When you are doing deals, don't just think about the short-term gain; think strategically about the long-term big picture. Is this deal taking you where you want to go? I don't mean being fussy about who you sell to, but making sure you know who the big players are in your field and where the money is going to come from.

Business savvy

Thinking on your feet and reinventing the rules

If you can get hold of a big brand product and cut the price, you will sell shed-loads. It is quite another ballgame to introduce an unknown brand. It takes **lateral thinking and a lot of determination** to recreate the market-place and to convince every potential purchaser not just that 'I want one of those', but that 'I genuinely need one of those'.

And make no mistake – **you are a brand**, in the same way that your product or your service is a brand.

If you are on a limited budget and you need to shift stock or get noticed fast, there is no substitute for personal contact. Retail selling? Get to the most senior decision-maker as fast as you can. Direct selling? Don't be passive – be active – get on the phone, seek out face-to-face meetings, get a

'My involvement in *The Apprentice*
showed me that I can be more
pushy than I would be naturally ...'

AN APPRENTICE

sale there and then, and leave your customer with an incentive to get others to buy too.

Stymied by bureaucracy or the way things are 'always done'? Frustrated and hampered by 'the rules'? Then be determined to reinvent the methodology. I'm not proposing all-out anarchy here. Bucking the system won't get you anywhere. You have to work within it to begin with. But industries, like businesses, get stuck in a rut, and **if something is not getting through because the system is in the way, the system may be outdated.**

Don't waste your time with blockers and jobs-worths, but don't alienate them either because they will just become more entrenched in their attitudes. Use them to get to where you need to be. You may have to operate outside your comfort zone, but take appropriate action to **make sure you are dealing with decision-makers** at the right level to get things achieved; and please note – this does not necessarily mean the person at the top.

There are shelf-loads of books on successful sales techniques, and directories full of training courses on how to open and close a deal. I will not go into the detail of that here – although if you watch *The Apprentice* you will pick up a lot of practical insight. The point is, you need to stay sharp, you need to stay focused, you need to remember that whatever your sector, profit is the bottom line. The candidates who succeeded never forgot that they were there to win – that they had to keep thinking on their feet and keep on selling – because there was a team of competitors on their tails just dying to see them get fired! **Think survival**. It's a jungle out there, and you need to know that you have the skills to survive if you were lost and starving; and that others want, need and depend upon you to survive.

Take action

- Understand your client base. Ask questions. Find out about the structure and size of the company, and, if necessary, check their credit rating. You need to make sure they can pay you.
- Make sure you know who you are talking to, what their role is within the organization, who they report to and whether they are able to make decisions.
- There are jobs-worths and action blockers in every organization, and sometimes they have very charming faces. If you're not getting the result you need, find out who you should be talking to and deal with them instead. Note: the person at the top is not necessarily the decision-maker for your product or service; they too can be a blocker if they don't understand the value of what you're offering.
- Remember that you've got a business to run. By all means do people favours, but not at the expense of your own or your employer's profit or survival. (That is especially true if you have employees or a team reporting to you.)

Flexibility

The willingness to learn from others and keep an open mind

Flexibility is the key to survival in business. It is crucial to stay flexible because things change: trends, markets, technology – everything changes, and so do we. I change because I am still learning. I learn new skills every day; I learn things, good and bad, from everyone I meet. Learning is what keeps us flexible, keeps creativity alive; it is what links generations together and allows us to survive.

'Reaching a consensus regarding
something that is innately creative
is extremely challenging.'
AN APPRENTICE

Change also means that the marketplace will want something from you tomorrow that is different from the product or service you are providing today. It is up to you to find a way of providing it – profitably.

The language of the modern world is different from the language that I grew up with. The vocabulary has changed, and the business processes are different too. On the one hand, business is more formal – a handshake is no longer enough to secure a firm deal; on the other hand, everything is more large-scale and fast-moving.

Each of the Apprentices was forced to **be flexible in order to survive**. They were tested to their limits in the various scenarios and business situations that were set for them in the tasks of *The Apprentice* series. Many later cited flexibility as one of the most crucial skills that they had learned.

Take action
- Make sure you are not being rigid in your approach. Having fixed ideas about how things should be done and completely overruling your team's objections is no way to run a business. **If you're being rigid, you're not listening. If you're not listening, you won't survive.**
- Be aware of what the rest of your market is doing: note changes in pricing, distribution, product features, fashion, lifestyle – and make sure you are ahead in your game.
- Know your weaknesses as well as your strengths, and instead of being defensive about them, bring on board others who can help you achieve your endgame. Adapting is the key to survival.

Millionaire mentality
Respect the bottom line

You don't have to be a millionaire to adopt a millionaire mentality, but without it you're unlikely to become one. I didn't start life with the aim of becoming a millionaire. I became self-employed in order to be in control of my own destiny and because I could see a way to make more money than if I stayed working as an employee. **Millionaires are financially aware**: they are aware of the value of their time, of the fact that **margin is more important than cash-in-hand at the end of the day**.

Entrepreneurs who start a business must do so with a **personal payday** in mind. By that I mean that you are in business to make money and you must always charge appropriately for your product, your service and for your time. In a start-up business, however, the owner may not expect to pay themselves a salary in the first year because all profits are channelled back into the business to help it to grow. A personal payday is important because it is a sign that you are being financially astute – and the business is making a profit.

It is difficult to take money out of the business when you want to safeguard the future wellbeing of the company. If you can channel it back into the business, you will reap dividends further down the line. I have no problem with spending millions on merchandise, plant and equipment, but I can't bear waste.

I can't stress enough how important it is not to borrow money if you can avoid it – and certainly not at start-up stage. Planning is essential, but too much time spent on honing a theoretical business plan and not enough on selling will simply stymie development.

> 'Each task was designed to
> expose a raw business skill.'
> **AN APPRENTICE**

So often there is too much focus on the financial theory and not enough energy going into growing the business. In the early days of growth, any kind of loan can leave your business vulnerable. It is one of the ironies of the business world that if a company owes £50,000 because it has over-stretched itself, the bank will have no hesitation in foreclosing on the loan, selling the company assets to get back £40,000 and writing off £10,000. But if you owe £100 million, it is a different ball game – it becomes a matter for the financial advisers, who are able to represent the bottom line in a way that will attract new investors to the failing business. One thing is certain: advisers will never let you down when there is a fat fee involved.

So I **keep a close eye on the bottom line at all times**. Margin is king as far as I am concerned. I invest profits wisely, and I safeguard the future wealth of my family and associates by keeping the speculative side of my business separate from a more safe and secure property portfolio.

This was one of the key elements that I was interested in when appraising the performance of the Apprentices. Would they remember what they were trying to achieve? Was profit, or service, or quality the true driver? The product design and farmers' market tasks (see pages 155 and 188) were particularly interesting for this. On the other hand, the art challenge task (page 172) involved a major moral dilemma. Would the teams behave ethically and ensure that the desire to win or the desire for money didn't lead them to step across personally acceptable boundaries?

Take action
- Are you living beyond your means? There is nothing wrong with aspiring to a better lifestyle, but if you're spending money that you don't have, your profits will be feeding the

bank's profit margins, not your own.
- 'Buy low, sell high' is the first rule of business, especially when creating a new product and establishing your profit margins.
- **Never forget what your time is worth to your business,** and don't squander it.

> '*The Apprentice* stretched my abilities –
> and I learnt a lot about myself.'
>
> **AN APPRENTICE**

Have you got the stamina for success?

I have worked hard from the day I took my first job until the present. Call it a work ethic if you like – instilled from an early age by a family that worked very, very hard. I know that I could be a workaholic, but fortunately my family would never stand for that, and the electronic revolution means that it is now possible to stay in touch with the international markets without having to sit by the telephone at three o'clock in the morning.

To be successful you need to have stamina, you need to be physically and mentally fit, you need to be able to cope with immense levels of pressure without losing your cool – and **you need to be rigorously well-disciplined**. I believe in leading by example, and if I'm not driven and well organized myself, how can I expect my staff to be?

For me, Monday to Friday means intensive work. I work flat out from the time I arrive at the office until the time I go home. In fact, I suffer a kind of guilt sometimes, a ridiculous guilt, if for some reason I find myself returning home early one evening. I'll stalk and storm around the house until about seven o'clock, when my body clock tells me, 'All right – you're at home now'. It's the guilt of not being at work. However, I also believe in the importance of family and achieving a balance. Weekends have always been my own. It's the time when I rest. It's the time when I have the human equivalent of a 5000-mile service, if you like. If I'm feeling relaxed and healthy in mind and body when I start work on Monday morning, I can cope with whatever the week throws at me.

The Apprentices would need all their stamina over the intensive 12 weeks that they were working on my tasks. They were eating, drinking, talking, waking and sleeping *The Apprentice*. Stamina played a key part in their survival. One candidate acknowledged a recognition that just because they could work through until three in the morning with no problem, it did not mean that others could, and that they needed to take account of the needs of the rest of the team in order for them all to perform at optimum capacity.

Focus and discipline
Success needs your personal commitment
I am a highly disciplined person. My time has value, and I calculate what that value is. Therefore it is critical that I spend my time focused on those things that are the best use of my time and deliver the most effective results.

Anything that is not the best use of my time I delegate. The ability to delegate effectively and to work in partnership with others in business is important in getting the job done both effectively and efficiently. It is a skill that some of the Apprentices had to learn the hard way!

One of the problems among those people, especially young people, who believe they want to go into business on their own is that they have a vision of a life of freedom and luxury – of living life at the top with all the nice things that go with it. They see themselves sitting behind a desk with their feet up, dishing out instructions. The hard lesson is that they're totally and absolutely wrong. If being in charge of an empire is their motivation for going it alone, they'll be doing it for the wrong reasons because it's not like that at all. In fact, you work much, much harder for yourself than you do for anybody else; and it takes time to get to the top.

Success needs your personal commitment – to keep your eye on the game when the going gets tough; to recognize that you have staff whose

'You don't have to be the brightest
button in the pack to be successful.'
AN APPRENTICE

livelihood depends upon your success. And once you're successful, to be aware that the economy may be affected by your changes in direction, or poor judgement on the part of senior management.

Take action

- Take a good, hard look at your strengths and weaknesses. If your weaknesses include putting things off, doing things late, sitting in front of the television instead of getting on with other priorities, you'll have to work pretty hard to take control of your time and change those lazy habits in order to succeed.
- If you're the kind of person who is always on the go, always has a project in hand and has an energy and a buzz, you're starting out with the right attitude. The question is, are you focusing your energies on your business niche?
- The flip side of this is achieving a balance. There is no point in driving yourself into the ground. If you always have a mountain of paper on your desk at the end of the day and find others are always delegating to you instead of the other way around, you need to assert yourself more and focus on planning. Better planning means you can delegate more effectively and make optimum use of your day (see pages 108 and 112).

Negotiation skills
Deal outside your comfort zone in order to win
Negotiating is really a part of selling – and selling is part of everyday life. It is about winning, about projecting the positive side of your nature, and it is also about taking control, about holding your nerve beyond the point of normal comfort when you want to achieve something. But comfort zones can change depending upon what you are negotiating. There are things

'There is always room to negotiate!'

AN APPRENTICE

we are comfortable negotiating for – the price of a second-hand car, for example; and things that may cause embarrassment or awkwardness, such as negotiating a reduction in dental charges or your gas bill.

If you want something desperately enough, you will go to the wall for it – and in reality everything is up for negotiation. Interestingly, though, not everyone is willing to try or even to succeed. They get uncomfortable when the person they are negotiating with gets tetchy; they take a 'no' at face value and won't work at turning it around; they will apologize before asking deeper questions, and look obviously uncomfortable at being forthright. People like that should not be in sales – and if they are would-be entrepreneurs, they had better get a good salesperson on their team to counter-balance their reticence to have even the slightest chance of succeeding.

Good negotiation may take patience, it may take pushiness, but most of all **it takes personality and intuition** – to know when to push for the hard sell, and when to hold back, not to appear too anxious, to wait, and wait and wait … interminably sometimes … for the phone call that says you have clinched the deal. As long as the person you are speaking to does, on some level, want to buy, a negotiation is always possible.

Those who are less likely to succeed in selling are the ones who are too polite or too embarrassed to ask the straight questions, who haven't got the tenacity to keep beating away the obstacles. They may close the deals – eventually – but the odds of success are reduced and they are less likely to make high margins. Selling and negotiating were at the root of all the tasks set for the Apprentices. They also had to learn how to adjust personal style, depending upon the market sector they were pitching to.

Take action

- Do you enjoy the buzz of a good deal? Look at what makes you stop negotiating, and push yourself to be even tougher. The more you stretch the boundaries of your personal comfort zone, the more successful you will be.
- Realize that everything you do in life, from discussing who should do the washing-up to finding out whether the person you are attracted to will go out with you, is potentially a negotiation.
- Learn to read body language, and see what it takes to close a deal when a discussion drags on and on to no avail.
- Next time you're faced with a no in business, do what it takes to convert it to a yes, even if you are inwardly cringing with discomfort. The triumph of success will cure you forever.

Persistence

Have the tenacity to keep going against all odds

Persistence implies overcoming obstacles, and you will have gathered by now that I am a believer in the value of learning from the school of hard knocks. Difficulty and adversity really can make you stronger if you have the grit to keep on trying. All **success comes from learning**. And to learn you need to begin by trying, and trying usually means making mistakes – lots of them.

In my experience, all the successes in my businesses evolved from learning what *not* to do. You learn what not to do because you tried it once before and it didn't work. You also learn when you are knocked back hard that you are made of sterner stuff than you realized – and that not only can you survive, but also that you are stronger as a result. Sadly, not all the Apprentices could stay to the end of the 12-week job interview process, but I am confident that each of them will have learned new skills.

To **keep going against all odds** you've got to love what you do, you need to be fairly pig-headed in your determination, and you need to be very, very honest with yourself.

To keep yourself motivated **when things go wrong**, you need to analyze where things went wrong. You have to be very realistic. Don't try to blame the rest of the world. **The blame lies only with you**. Recognize that immediately. You also need a contingency plan.

If a particular project has gone wrong and you can see the reasons why, it might be a case of giving it up forever, or it might be a case of developing your idea differently, or revisiting the costs. While operating on gut instinct may be fine as far as product development is concerned, at Amstrad we learnt early on not to be tempted to let our enthusiasm take over and lead us into the common mistake of making or buying too much stock before selling even one unit. These days we might take a bit of a punt to begin with, but in general we don't get it wrong any more. We're more careful now.

Persistence is a critical skill in business. There is no such thing as overnight success. We're all in it for the long game, and that takes strategic planning and determination to succeed. If you haven't got those characteristics, stick to the day job.

Take action

- Don't be a quitter and don't blame others. Take stock, then knuckle down and get on with the job.
- Single-minded determination feeds self-belief and will help you eventually to win through. Break the obstacle down into composite pieces and tackle them **one step at a time**.

> 'A "can do" attitude is vitally
> important in business ... you can do
> anything you put your mind to.'
>
> **AN APPRENTICE**

- You can be sure that whatever obstacles you are facing, others have faced similar things and have come through them, and you will face much bigger obstacles in the future. **Recognize what is in your control and do something about it. Recognize what is outside your control and work around it.**

Hunger for the next challenge

Enjoy turning opportunities into realities

I am often asked when I will stop, at what point I will step away from what I have created, saying 'Enough is enough'. The truth is that I can't envisage such a time. I can't imagine not being excited by the buzz of the next opportunity and not having the enthusiasm to develop the idea. One of the things I value most about the culture created in my companies is the **energy** that is present. We are able to move fast when we have an idea, we can make things happen, we can influence the marketplace (provided we have done our research). There is a hunger for the new and a dread of stagnation, of standing in one place, or letting others overtake us. The hunger is linked to **the will to win**, but it is also linked to a love of the task and of the industry that we're in.

True leadership is energetic and enthusiastic – it makes things happen. It is what enables you to bounce back after a string of defeats, rejuvenated by a good night's sleep and say, 'OK, bring on the next challenge'.

Sticking with it and being enthusiastic can be tough. It was interesting to see whether any of the Apprentices would give up – perhaps the prospect of working for me was too daunting! Perhaps the process of filming and being apart from friends and family would take its toll. When you are working hard to make your dream business successful, you may not have as much contact with – and time to spend with – family and friends as you would like, and dividing your time or **feeling alone can affect your performance**. Just as the Apprentices found this a difficult aspect of making a TV series and completing the tasks, it is also a difficult aspect of leading a team in business.

Losing your hunger for your work needn't threaten your future, provided you are not running your own show. If you are running your own show, there are others depending on you, and you need to keep that hunger and energy alive, or to hand over the creative reins to someone else who is still buzzing at the idea of doing something new.

Hunger is the characteristic that will enable you to overcome obstacles, to think laterally to solve problems and to believe you have the ability to succeed.

A hunger for the next challenge is a key characteristic in those with entre-preneurial personalities: they are always seeing possibilities where no one else can see them. If you have that hunger in you, do all you can to nurture it in either your business or your personal life. It is a gift that will keep you searching, growing and learning.

Take action
- Love what you do and do what you love, otherwise you will become unhappy and self-defeating.
- If you enjoy what you do, don't be afraid of expressing your enthusiasm. Enjoyment is infectious and you will bring others along with you.
- A product that has the heart of the team it is likely to be a better product; it will be more in tune with the market's requirements

'Look at what you've achieved
in life and be confident that
you made it possible.'

AN APPRENTICE

and it will perform ahead of the competition.
- Recognize your own entrepreneurial spirit and make sure you feed yourself new challenges.

Courage
Have the guts to succeed

Success isn't just about being good enough – it's about **taking a chance**, taking a gamble, seeing an opportunity and **having the guts to go for it** – to enter into uncharted territory. It can also mean forcing others to sit up and pay attention, rather than accepting their nos at face value.

In Amstrad's early days we were battling to get the retail giant Comet to take our amplifiers. I could not persuade them to take stock, so I had to find something that Gerry Mason, Comet's then marketing director, wanted so that I could **gain bargaining power**. They needed Garrard record players at increased discount. I managed to secure a deal. Gerry was delighted, and although I still didn't get an order, I won a listing in the Comet adverts that were seen nationally by the public.

Then came the main chance: I encouraged friends and family around the UK to place orders for the amplifiers – and finally, the call came. Comet had received orders for seven of our amplifiers and would therefore take 10 to be on the safe side. **I blew a carefully calculated gasket.** I knew how they operated. Ten amplifiers meant no repeat orders or roll-out to the main stores. I told them, 'You're Comet! You're not taking an order for 10 units; you've got to take at least 100 or it's ridiculous.'

Since then, we've never looked back, and the relationship between Comet and Amstrad flourished.

Some would say I conned them. In fact, **I helped them to make a highly lucrative decision**.

You'll never be successful if you're cautious. That's why accountants are accountants, engineers are engineers, lawyers are lawyers. The engineer who distracts himself into becoming a businessman is less likely to succeed. He is a different animal. However, nothing is written in stone. If there were rules that we could all follow, there would be lots more multi-millionaires out there in the world. One of the characteristics I liked most about the Apprentices was their courage. Their courage in coming on the show, their courage in taking on whatever tasks were thrown at them, and most of all their courage in facing me – the man with a reputation for being blunt and brutal – and the prospect of being fired, in spite of their best efforts.

Take action
- If you've got an idea you believe in, come up with a strategy to sell it, whether to your corporate bosses, to your marketplace or to another company. Nothing will happen to move your idea ahead unless you are behind it 200 per cent.
- Play the game. If you have spotted a market niche for your product and you can't persuade the buyers to take it, find something else that they do want and use that as a bargaining point to achieve your true objective.
- Test yourself at every opportunity. Feeling shy about talking to someone influential? Decide what you need to say and just say it. Uncertain about how the marketplace operates? Find someone who does know and ask questions. Need to shift some stock? Get out into the market and sell face to face, or look into bulk selling via other means.

'Be yourself at all times.'
AN APPRENTICE

Can you lead from the front?

Leading from the front is easiest if you surround yourself with a team of people who share your beliefs and values and whom you can trust. This is easier to achieve in the early days of starting up a company than later on when the corporation is larger. Once you begin to delegate the task of recruitment to others in the organization, there is no longer any guarantee that you will get to know the individuals concerned. In order to lead it is critical that you are seen, and that your staff know you are not only present, but also that you are interested in – and make it your business to know – what is going on.

You have the vision. It is up to you to communicate that vision to your team clearly and concisely, in a manner that is understood; to delegate effectively and to ensure that you follow through in such a way that individuals take responsibility for their own actions; and to keep it that way. It looks so easy written on the page, but for many people leadership and management are the most difficult areas of running a business to tackle. These sections are intended to give you some insight into the way I approach my role.

Leadership
Self-management and the importance of being yourself
A leader needs others to follow in order to achieve an objective. That's what a leader is for. A good leader is not necessarily always the most well-liked person in the company, but the best ones are liked because they are respected for their **clarity and vision**.

Leaders tend to be born rather than made, although it's true to say that some people grow into a leadership role later on in their careers. Effective leadership is about earning respect, and it's also about personality and

> 'A good leader needs to learn to step
> back because others have good ideas too.'
>
> **AN APPRENTICE**

charisma. If you want to be everyone's best friend, it will be hard for you to make it in business.

Inspiring others is important, but if you're leading from the front, you also need to **inspire yourself**, and to inspire yourself you need to understand what motivates you to succeed. That was quite a challenge to the Apprentices, as each was a follower one day and a leader the next.

In my case it is easy. I am motivated by making a profit, the buzz of the deal and an enthusiasm for innovation – being first in the marketplace with a life-changing product. My personal style is well known. I am upfront, belligerent if necessary, with high expectations, and I do my best to lead by example. My style is also inclusive, however, and I am a great believer in making sure that everyone knows what is going on, and that credit is given where it is due.

In order to gain respect you need to **be true to yourself**. There is no point in trying to be brutal if it's not in your nature; there is no point in trying to be suave and sophisticated if it doesn't come naturally. In business, as in life, people like to know who they are dealing with. **No one trusts a faker**.

In business, as in friendships, there is a getting-to-know-you process. Focus first on achieving a successful outcome from the business task in hand, and the liking may follow – as a bonus.

Take action
- Pay attention to the sections on communication and delegation (pages 105–8 and 112–14), the two foundation stones upon which good leadership and management are based.

- Don't try to be something you're not – but at the same time be sure to work on those skills that undermine your ability to earn respect from your team.
- Be particular about who you employ, making sure they can be trusted and that they will suit the personality of the organization.
- Plan ahead and be disciplined in your approach to self-managment. It is hard to earn the respect of others if you do not practise what you preach.

Planning and adapting
Organizing the organization
There's no point in asking an entrepreneur what he plans to do next, or whether he visualizes achieving a certain level of success by a certain date. It's like asking a songwriter, 'At what point did you decide you were going to write your next song?' It doesn't work like that. It just happens; it's a natural desire to go ahead and do something else, to move on. Once you've succeeded in achieving one goal, you go on and do other things, mainly product-orientated. It's simply that once you get on a roll, you're on a roll, and you just keep on rolling. You **go with the momentum**. You don't just stop.

I've always broken the rules, especially within Amstrad, and we really don't have the conventional corporate structure that you would find in many large companies. I personally feel that if you were to ask every fund manager who has ever invested in Amstrad for their concern about the company, it would not be whether I am going to do something silly and lose all their money, whether I'm going to do something mad and bankrupt the company. Their concern is more likely to be that I am the company: 'What happens if Sugar gets run over by a bus?'

We won't impose a structure because we want to retain the flexibility to communicate fast and act quickly.

Project planning is important, but it's also important not to become so caught up in your own business plan that you don't act, or stick to the plan so rigidly that you don't adapt.

Each industry has its own rhythm, its own pattern, its own market expectations. The big difference between the tasks set for the Apprentices and what *I* do in the real world, is timing. We're open for business all day, every day, all year round. There's no set timeframe for action.

Planning a product as far as I'm concerned is a **continual process**.

I do not pre-set targets that state we *must* launch one product a week, or we *must* launch one product a month. We might not bring out a new product for two years, or we might bring five out in one year. We react to the way the market is moving and what the market needs. Everything we do is market-driven, and in the case of *my* companies, it's all technology-driven. Rather than bring out a new model of a product for the sake of it, we keep on selling – we sell it to the death. There's no time limit on anything. As long as the market wants it, they'll keep getting it and we'll keep on marketing it.

If a product is doing very well, our aim becomes to **enhance the margin**. Typically, in the electronics industry, something that starts off costing a certain amount to produce will come down in price when the second lot is made. If your product is selling well at the price you launched it at, then by all means put the additional margin in your pocket. If it's not, think about rejuvenating the market for the product by dropping the price. Even though you're changing the price, there should still be the scope to increase your margin. This applies to selling a service too. Perceived value is important. Make sure you are not underselling yourself.

My aim has been to retain the quick-fire energy and ability to adapt that allows small start-up companies to succeed, while combining it with large-scale manufacturing capability.

There is a small, central, creative hub headed by me. The rest is to do with project management and product delivery. To impose management structure would be to slow down a working method that has its own shape and influence. I have seen too many entrepreneurial companies flattened by jargon and bureaucracy, so I was determined, following flotation, that that would not be the outcome with Amstrad.

Take action

- Assess whether your own decision-making system is effective or whether you need some additional expertise on board.
- Be aware of your management style. How do you organize, plan and make changes? Do you want regular, structured meetings, or will the team operate more creatively and effectively without being hamstrung by bureaucratic structures?
- Focus on designing and delivering the products effectively. In my view everything else is peripheral to that and can be sorted out as and when necessary.
- Be extremely organized where finance is concerned, make sure you are not under- or over-pricing your product or services, and ensure you have excellent advisers.

Focusing on finance
Never borrow what you can't repay

I never had any money when I was starting out. My business has always been run on what I can finance myself. Now, as then, profits are ploughed into the business as soon as they are made, which allows me to do more. Now, of course I have used the facility of the bank's overdraft, but I've always treated it as a fallback. Overdrafts are for certain times of the year when you are building up stocks and inventory – you need help to finance that – but it's short-term finance because you see it quickly turn back into the black. It's vitally important in my view not to get third-party finance. **Being lean forces you to stretch yourself.** It focuses you. It keeps your eye on the ball.

I subscribe to the train of thought that says: if you want finance, what are you going to put up to the bank? Why should the bank take a risk on you? **There are no free lunches in this world.** It doesn't help to moan about banks and financial institutions that you think should be in awe of your business plan. The chances are that the only one in awe of your business plan is you. Why should they give you any money? They don't owe you any-thing. If you don't have collateral and you haven't proved yourself in the market yet, you are a risk – to yourself as well as to the financial institutions.

So, start small. Start with a limited amount of your own finance. When you start to make profits, and when you can show a healthy balance sheet – after two or three years – then you might get the bank's attention; then you might get a financier's attention. But if you're looking for someone to finance you in the short-term, you'd better see your mum or your uncle or (and I don't recommend this one) rob a bank. No one else is going to give it to you. It is no use trying to run, in financial terms, before you can walk.

People want to be big, they want to be successful; they think of an idea on Monday and they want it to happen by Friday. But, unfortunately, life doesn't work that way.

There's nothing wrong with being optimistic about your plans and out- wardly buoyant, so long as you are personally counting the beans. By all means try to stimulate enthusiasm and be positive, but to be successful you have to remain down-to-earth and realistic yourself.

Each of the tasks set for the Apprentices involved a budgetary element. How they spent their seed money contributed to their overall success.

Take action

- Work within what you have financially – not within what you would like to have.
- Do plan your budget, but don't expect any large-scale investments from a third-party financier until you have proved yourself to be a safe bet.
- Start small and grow; it will allow you to develop more solidly and learn from your experience rather than your mistakes.
- Make sure you are on good financial terms with your suppliers and retailers at all times, but maintain the possibility of being flexible if their goods or the discount structures become prohibitively expensive.

Communication skills

How to communicate your ideas

Communication is critical to the effective running of a successful company. It's vital to convey information quickly and effectively. It is an obvious thing to say, but it's important that everyone knows:

- What is going to happen,
- When it's going to happen,
- Why it's happening,
- Who is responsible for making it happen,
- What the expected outcome will be.

The message needs to **be concise, precise and to the point**. Get the facts out, don't cloud the issue, don't try to be too clever, get the bullet points across – and look at the person you're talking to. If they still look a bit confused, go down a level in your explanation – especially if you're starting to bombard them with technicalities.

I am the kind of person who keeps on the move, so I do speak to a lot of my staff every day. But some employees work off-site or in another time zone, so I make it my policy to keep in touch by email: brief, concise and to the point.

I have no patience with those who claim not to know what is going on, and I have no respect for managers and leaders who do not communicate properly. We are surrounded by Star Wars' technology that allows easy communication anywhere, any time and with anybody.

Speaking to people face to face is usually the preferred and most effective method of communication, but that is not always possible or realistic. Phone calls are more personal than email, but impractical on a large-scale basis and potentially time-consuming. Meetings have their own agenda.

There are far too many rules bandied about regarding how to conduct meetings. Most of them are utter nonsense. You cannot generalize about

'Effective networking is important
in business and maintaining good
contacts is invaluable.'
AN APPRENTICE

the size or frequency of meetings. They are as large or as small as they need to be. Sometimes there are only one or two people present; sometimes there are 30. If we're briefing a whole team of people about a new product, or finding out the progress of something that's involves 15 people, they *all* need to be there.

Communication, leadership and project management go hand in hand. You can't simply communicate your ideas once and expect everyone to act on them in unison. Communication is about keeping in touch – with your staff, with the marketplace, with your external suppliers – and it is about all parties taking responsibility for keeping each other informed.

Just as one of the challenges of running a creative business is to judge the right moment to launch a new idea, so too is it important to decide when to invest in new communication technology. There are those among my staff, and some cheeky journalists with long memories, who will remember that back in 1993 I made a statement during the filming of a BBC television documentary to the effect that my staff would not be using email. These days that may seem absurd, but at the time it was the right call. There was no point in my businesses using email if the rest of the world was still sending faxes and telexes to communicate with each other. The commercial world depends upon precise information changing hands fast, and by proven reliable methods. Email was a risk at the time.

The good news is that the Internet and technology are now used extensively around the world and I am able to communicate from a central point to everywhere and everybody that I deal with.

Take action

- If you've got something to say, say it. Don't worry about composing a lengthy memo that is word perfect but that no one will read. Communicate concisely, effectively and promptly in order to transmit your idea.
- Don't censor information unless it is highly confidential. Your team will be much more cooperative if they feel included in what is going on.
- Keeping people informed is not the same as giving each person a say in the decision-making process. Keep your door open to feedback, but make it clear who is the decision-maker for the task.
- If you are leading a project don't rely on a single communication to get the job done. Combine the written with the personal and make sure all parties know what they are meant to achieve and by when.

Managing time

How to make maximum use of your most valuable resource

My motto is: 'Always **clear your desk, every day**.' I never leave any paperwork on my desk at the end of the day because doing so means that something is being put off, that a decision is being delayed. It is an ethos that I try to instill in the rest of my team. I become very frustrated if things aren't done when I expect them to be.

Do not put off messages, answers and decisions – they've got to be dealt with one day. It's a bit like your gas bill or electricity bill. You leave it hanging around, but you know you've got to pay it, so you might as well pay it straight away. That's my philosophy. Bang – in comes a question from a member of my staff. Bang – there goes the answer back straight away. Obviously that can't be done on every occasion, but I try. It's a kind of discipline.

It annoys me tremendously when people I deal with do not follow the same policy – not prioritizing in the correct order, not getting things done, putting off decisions, thinking that they'll get around to it another time. The thing that irritates me the most is having to ask people why they haven't done something and listening to the excuse, 'Well, I was going to do it tomorrow'. It's an answer that doesn't go down very well with me when I want an answer now – and I always want things done now!

Of course you can't apply this philosophy to everything – but it's the sense of urgency, the use of time that is important.

Time is the biggest asset I have in respect to interfacing with the outside world as well. As far as international business is concerned, dealing with America or the Far East, for example, I could easily be at work 24 hours per day. In running my business, it is part of my job to 'keep the plates spinning' so that other people can get on with their work too. I have to provide the people in the Far East with enough information for their 8 a.m. start so they can get on with the job and will be able to give me answers later in the day. It's no good leaving them up in the air, because there's a time difference that could potentially be costly when the rest of their world is closed.

The same applies to staff in the UK offices. The person at the top needs to be ahead of the game, blazing the trail for the next action, the next strategic move. I guess you could say that I keep everybody on their toes.

Time was possibly the greatest challenge for the Apprentices because each of the tasks was tightly time-bound. There were no extensions possible! This forced some tight and creative solutions and enabled several candidates to break free of previous slower-moving habits of decision-making.

Take action

- Time management is linked to self-discipline and needs a robust approach to both planning and delegation. It's a valuable commodity, and planning your time will help you to be more focused and help clarify priorities.
- Be rigorous in your approach to your 'in' tray, and be clear as to your own core skills. Be aware if you are doing a job that could be one just as effectively (albeit not in quite the same way) by someone else.
- Avoid self-indulgence. Don't get distracted by personal emails, and if possible make sure all emails are screened by a third party so you see only the essentials.
- Learn to delegate (see page 112). You may need to take time out to train someone, not once, not twice, but six or 10 times. However, once they understand your requirements, you will become twice as effective and they will have learnt a new skill.

Motivational style

Inspiring your team to deliver and to succeed

Motivation is all about inspiring people. Your team may consist of just you and one other person, but there is probably a whole host of other people in the supply chain who may or may not feel part of what is going on, and may or may not feel appreciated.

Sometimes the people you need to inspire are remote from the centre of decision-making, so they might not feel the same sense of 'ownership' of the project as its main creators. Designers, engineers and manufacturers are often divorced from the final result, and consequently also divorced from the final success of the project.

'You can learn an enormous
amount in a team environment
where all skills are respected.'
AN APPRENTICE

I will sometimes use my time to explain to these vital participants in the process: 'Do you realize that you are working on something here that is far superior to anything else in the marketplace? And if my gut feeling is right, when it gets out there it's going to be a winner, and when you walk down the high street with your children at the weekend, you'll look in that shop and you'll say, "I made that, you know, I'm a part of that". Or "I made the software", or "I designed it", "I drew it", "I actually manufactured it", "I loaded it on a lorry", "I delivered it"...' I think it's very important that people such as software engineers and mechanical engineers, who do specific tasks to make specific parts, are not left in isolation, but understand what they are doing their jobs for.

They also get to hear: 'This product is late because *you* didn't do this ...' or 'This product is going to be ready because you *did* do this'. **I motivate, but I'm also honest about situations.** And as the Apprentices got to know each other they really came to value the ability of their team members to motivate them through the rougher, tougher moments.

Take action
- Be aware of how far your team extends – from the receptionist who is the public face of the company to the warehouse operator who needs to deliver stock on time, to the retailer who is handling orders from a multitude of other customers, or, in the case of a smaller operation, to your neighbour who has the kindness to take delivery of a heavy parcel when you are out. Make sure they understand their part in the process and are appreciated.
- Be consistent. Everyone has off-days, but the office is no place to vent your anger at a personal crisis or to take out on your colleagues the fact that you are not feeling very well.

- Stay positive. Even if you are annoyed, make sure you are focused on the art of the possible and encourage everyone to keep working towards achieving a common goal and a positive outcome.
- Don't humiliate people in front of their colleagues. If you've got something to say, blame them in their professional capacity; don't be tempted to insult the person.
- Stay well-motivated yourself. Make sure you keep your eyes fixed firmly on the goal and do not get distracted by peripherals.

Delegation

Remember to trust your staff and not do their jobs for them

The secret of delegation is to make sure you are delegating the right tasks and to follow through on them. If you are the leader of an organization, it is a poor use of your time to do administrative tasks. If you are the engineer, by all means make your suggestions to the marketing department, but don't start writing the advertising copy. If you are the project manager, don't start undermining your team by doing all the work yourself. You get the idea.

Taking on too many staff can be a mistake too. It's important not to over-invest in staff. Only take on new people when you have to. It affects your bottom line, and your overheads add up.

I took on my first employees in the early days so that I didn't have to spend my time packing parcels. Later, other facets of the business, such as doing the accounts, would be delegated. The company then got to a size where the organization of transport was becoming too time-consuming for me, so I had to get someone to do that as well, to leave me with the most important elements.

> 'Being assertive without becoming
> aggressive is a crucial skill to learn.'
>
> **AN APPRENTICE**

Delegation, for me, is to do with delegating the physical tasks that need to be performed throughout my business.

With the exception of some products in the audio range, I don't think I have ever delegated the responsibility of dreaming up a product. What I call the key, blockbuster products have all been down to me.

My philosophy is to **never ask someone to do something that you can't do yourself.** That's not everyone's philosophy, of course – and, importantly, it is not the same as trying to do the expert's job for them. I have enough proficiency in engineering to be able to sit with an engineer and collaborate with him or her. I have a reasonable grasp of what software is capable of doing, although I haven't got a clue how it does it. Software is my biggest challenge because I don't have a true understanding of how long it reasonably takes to create it. I therefore have to remember to keep off the backs of the software designers. In every other aspect of the business I have a great understanding.

If you look at most successful businesses, you will find that the person at the top of the tree has **a large portfolio of skills** in that particular business.

Time management is dealt with on pages 108–10, and it works in partnership with effective delegation. We have all seen newly appointed managers who have not yet grown into their roles, acting 'down' and creating havoc for the tier of staff below them by trying to do their jobs for them. By all means **share the benefit of your experience** and encourage people on their way, but don't take over. If you do, you'll end up doing everyone's job for them, which means you'll disappear under a mountain of paper with no one left to delegate to – and they may well have to start doing yours.

It would be interesting to see how each of the Apprentices chose to delegate and whether they followed through and managed the process effectively.

Take action

- Make sure there is an able person filtering your emails, and if you find it hard to delegate, make sure you choose the kind of person who is not afraid to point that out to you.
- Follow through on the task, and set time-bound target dates for completion. **Delegation is not the same as letting go.** It is about managing a task through a third party because your own time is better spent focused elsewhere. It is like having an additional arm, not cutting one off and hoping it will work without your brain to instruct it how to move.
- Be aware that your task may be delegated further, and make sure that the person who has taken responsibility for that action is also taking full responsibility for the consequences.
- Don't be tempted to take the task back if it hasn't been done exactly to your specification. Brief the person you have asked to do the task and get them to alter it to your requirements.
- Be clear and concise, making sure that the person has understood fully, and don't apologize for giving them their job to do.

Valuing change
The importance of being adaptable

As Charles Darwin proved over a century ago, we need to **adapt in order to survive**. Nowhere is this truer than in business.

I started off as a wholesaler and then became a manufacturer. Since working in manufacturing, Amstrad has evolved to take advantage of many changes in technology, developing products that have transformed the hi-fi industry, capitalized on the CB radio boom, worked in partnership to deliver satellite TV to the UK, and is now at the cutting edge of telecommunications. We intend to survive for many more years yet.

Being adaptable to change applies to creating, selling and marketing a product (more about that in Chapter 4). It also applies to project planning and team-working. The reason our company is able to **respond quickly** to changes in the marketplace is because of our flexibility. Many of the large conglomerates are hide-bound by bureaucracy and it can take an age for them to make a decision. In my companies we are able to move fast, and with the right products are able to gain the market advantage.

When assessing our Apprentices, I wanted to be sure that whoever we appointed was flexible in approach, a good listener, quick on the uptake and fast to see and respond to new opportunities.

Take action

- If you're getting too attached to your business plan and your spreadsheets, the chances are you're losing your nerve or are not thinking creatively enough. Plans should be made to explore whether an action can be taken, not as a straitjacket for non-action or prevarication.
- Flexibility implies an ability to listen and to take account of the opinions of others, which means a more rounded, better informed decision will result. If you find yourself saying 'no' as a knee-jerk response, think again and listen up – you might be told something useful.
- Flexibility is not the same as changing your mind or being indecisive.

Flexibility means being open to change if the market requires it in order to remain profitable and to survive and thrive. Use a flexible approach to make a better decision, not just *any* decision.

Managing people

How to know what is really going on

There are no formal management structures in my companies – much to the disapproval of many. I know what is going on partly because I have told people what to do, and ensured the team is in place to deliver, and partly because **I ask what's going on**. It's not always easy to implement but in theory it really is that simple.

I manage people by remaining focused on the task. Delivering the task is the result of **clear briefing**, effective delegation, time management and getting regular **progress reports**.

Obviously I am working with people, not robots, and the personal element comes into it too, but the greater the sense of urgency in a business and the more focused the task, the easier it is to **maintain control** because staff don't have time to be distracted or diverted into non-essential activities.

I'm not saying we haven't had our problems. When the pressure is on all kinds of behaviours raise their heads, but in general I find that direct questions will eventually get me the answers I need.

I am the inspiration in my company. Like it or not, that's the way it is. I manage the show, but I've got a lot of very good people around me who actually implement my plans.

> 'Recognize individuals' strengths
> and weaknesses and play to their
> strengths for the good of the team.'
> **AN APPRENTICE**

I wanted to see which of the Apprentices the rest of the candidates would turn to in times of trouble, and who had the inspiration to lead them to success. Those troubleshooters would be amongst my finalists, and one of them would be my winner.

Take action
- If you run a large team, make sure you have lieutenants you can trust and who are effective people managers.
- Ensure that you have briefed everybody fully and that everyone understands his or her role in the process.
- Use your skills in time management and delegation to ensure that you are getting the feedback you want from the team.
- Trust your instincts. If you are getting glib answers, or someone is evading a direct question, keep asking questions until you get to the truth.
- If you have a non-player in your team, find out what the problem is and either move them to a role that will play to their strengths, or help them to leave.

Inspiring loyalty and trust
Value your staff and they will buy into your vision
I said at the outset that **loyalty and trust** are important values in business. The marketplace is a battleground, and unless you go into battle with an army that backs you 100 per cent, you will lose. No matter how brilliant you are at planning, strategy, sales or marketing, you will fail.

I am extremely lucky to still have many of the people who were with me when I started out. My staff tend to stay either for 20 minutes or for 20 years!

'Make sure that the people
around you are smart.'

AN APPRENTICE

Loyalty and trust have to be earned, and that usually takes time. It is earned as a result of delivering on your promises, of saying what you mean, of leading from the front and of being supportive to staff during times of challenge. It is also born of including others in your vision of the future. All successes are a team effort. No one person can achieve all their aims on their own. Therefore the **rewards need to be shared**.

The challenge for the Apprentices was to create loyalty among their team-mates and to win the respect and support of the advisers assigned to the task, with no benefit of past history and no time to build a relationship. It was interesting to see how they persuaded people to help them achieve their goals and what kind of alliances built up within the teams over time.

Take action
- If you feel you are not respected as a team leader or project manager, and don't have your team's loyalty and trust, take a good hard look at yourself and figure out why. If you can't see if for yourself, ask the team – they'll soon tell you!
- **Be honest with your team**. You don't necessarily have to tell them everything that's going on, but be straight and don't fudge difficult issues.
- Never ask anyone to do something you wouldn't be willing to do yourself.
- Be willing to take tough decisions and don't hide behind excuses.
- Be inclusive in your praise as well as your criticism. If it was a team effort, acknowledge it as such – don't keep all the glory for yourself.

- If insubordination rears its head, find out why it has occurred and nip it in the bud.

Rewarding enterprise
Recognize success and ensure your staff benefit

Although I don't believe in heaping praise on people just for doing the job they are paid to do, I fervently believe that **people should be rewarded** materially for their efforts, recognized for their successes and that long-term loyalty and commitment to the job should offer financial gain.

There are many different ways of rewarding people, and every company is different and has different needs. Personal and team recognition are probably the greatest motivators there are and should never be under-estimated.

Of course, within the context of the TV series, the Apprentices were unable to reward each other materially, but it was interesting to see whether credit was given where it was due for hard work, and where it was given for loy-alty and personal support. The personal factor often came into the Appren-tices' decision when it came to electing who not to send to the boardroom, for possible elimination from the TV series. The supportive team member would often reap the reward for their support by not being selected for the boardroom.I wasn't impressed by this tactic!

Take action
- Review your staff's pay scales in much the same way as you would decide how much you could spend on a project. Begin with the margin and work backwards.
- What can you afford to pay? If the answer is 'not enough', you

will have to be creative and offer variables, such as flexi-time or part-time work, more holiday, etc.

- The more financially secure the company, the more able you are to look at long-term investments that could benefit loyal staff.
- Although everyone needs a salary cheque, the majority of people work because they enjoy the environment or the job. Never underestimate the power of peers and the effectiveness of being appreciated for a job well done.

Do you enjoy your life?

Although I am guilty of living to work, the person who does not **strike a balance** and have outside interests as well, is a very dull individual. It's true to say in my own case, however, that the boundaries between work and play tend to get blurred. That's why it is so important to enjoy what you do. Without that enjoyment you will lead a very unhappy life.

I have a strong interest in aviation and took up flying in the late 1970s: it's something I do to relax and I really enjoy it. More recently the business instinct kicked in when I recognized that the market was now ready for an executive air service. So I decided to start up an air charter company specializing in private aviation.

We currently have three large jets and a charter brokerage division, which enables us to extend the service beyond our own planes, so we act as a broker to arrange flights on others' planes as well. Why queue up for three hours at Heathrow when you can speed up the process by using a corporate jet? You'll still have to go through the necessary security procedures, but the process is faster and more personal.

The point is that at a relatively low start-up cost I saw a window of opportunity that crossed the work–leisure divide. We started the business in 2003, and early signs are that it is doing extremely well.

That said, it is not always a good idea to blur the boundaries between work and leisure. What is important is that you **enjoy what you do and do what you enjoy**. If you're not having fun while you work, you need to think seriously about changing what you are doing.

Enjoying the challenge
Love what you do and do what you love

The Amstrad culture is one that exists because of its innovation, because of its **fighting spirit** and because of its realism in understanding that we have great competitors among us. That is the spirit that is in this company, that has been in this company for over 30 years. If we were to remain in business and offer just what everyone else offers, we would be dead in the water.

We are not a giant organization. We are a small cog in a giant wheel of an industry. We exist by fighting the big boys, and by using the flexibility that we enjoy as a medium-sized company and that the large companies can't have. Lack of speed is their Achilles heel. Why can't they do things? Because they're slow, they're lethargic. Amstrad is fast. We're on to things quickly. We maintain a quickness, a fast 'in and out' culture.

I am a great believer in sticking to what you know. Had I not liked the elec-tronics industry when I first got into it, I would have got out fast. I like this business. It's fast and it's exciting. You never know what is going to come next, what is going to be developed next.

Anyone in business has to enjoy what they do. I am fortunate that my employees share my **enthusiasm** for this business – especially the ones who have been with me a long time.

Some years ago someone described what we do as 'the Amstrad Effect'. That's a great compliment. I can't remember who said it, but it means bringing out something new, something that changes the world, changes the face of business. That's what I strive to do. That's what Amstrad is about and it's one of the things I love most about the business.

> 'Although being successful in
> business is vitally important, family
> and friends are important too.'
>
> **AN APPRENTICE**

The candidates impressed me with their ability to rise to each challenge; I wanted to know which of them was actually *enjoying* the process!

Take action

- If you're aiming to be a part of a large organization, ask some hard questions about whether it is the right corporate culture for you. Unless there are good reasons for them, frequent job changes on your CV raise more questions than they answer.
- If you're planning to start or grow your own business, make sure you know why you've chosen the sector you're in and check whether you enjoy what you do. If you're only in it for the financial opportunity, you'd better plan an exit strategy too.
- Understand your niche and where you fit in the marketplace. If you understand the rules of the game, you'll be better placed to win and take up a different position next time.

The bigger picture

Remember the life–work balance

I work hard and I play hard. It may sound like a cliché, but it's true. I start my day early and I work flat out. If I happen to find myself at home earlier than usual, I feel uncomfortable. The work ethic runs deep in my veins, and I don't think I'm going to change now.

But I have a family, too, and they are crucial to my happiness and my success. They are also part of my day, and I am a huge believer in **the importance of work–life balance.** Once I am at home they become my main focus.

The body is a different kind of machine from a computer. It wears out on a daily basis. It gets tired and it needs sleep. Creativity and originality need rest and nourishment. There's no point in becoming burnt out and dys-functional because your business and your staff will suffer. The bigger picture is about family, children, friends, community, the world at large – and enjoying and appreciating life.

Take action

- **You're not a machine**, and creativity and confidence can thrive only in a well-rested, well-nourished body. Be as rigorous in the way you manage your personal time as you manage your time at work, and remember to put your loved ones, not your profit margin, centre stage.
- Your mind is fed by a number of different influences, whether the buzz of a football match, the thrill of taking off in an aeroplane or listening to live music. You can only be in touch with what is happening in the marketplace if you are also in touch with the people who live in it. If you are glued to your desk seven days a week, get organized – and **get a life!**

Personal recognition
Enjoy celebrating your successes

I like to win – in business as well as in sport. When you reach a certain level of proficiency in sport you want to take on people you can try to beat and get better. But in business I don't mind being second, third or fourth because that also means doing very, very well. Sometimes you've got to be realistic. I'm not going to make more computers than IBM or Dell, and I'm not going to make more televisions than Sony – that would be ridiculous because the effort to lead the pack could also drive the company to failure. So if we make the third or fourth largest quantity, or even the tenth or whatever, that's great.

I value the recognition that I have earned, because I know how hard I and others in my companies have worked to achieve the level of success that we enjoy today, and I also know how far we have come. I choose not to live the lavish lifestyle, but there is no question that I live comfortably. I definitely find time to enjoy myself, and if I can find a way of doing some business at the same time, I will probably do that too.

Within *The Apprentice*, the treats enjoyed by the winning team at the end of each task were very much part of the incentive to participate – and they were all aiming for the final prize!

Staying the course and facing the threat of the boardroom were hard challenges for the Apprentices: the promise of final recognition was great but they were living a life for 12 weeks cut off from friends and family. It can be that way in business sometimes too – that is why getting on with your colleagues is important and why it is important to remain focused on what you are doing and to remember why you are doing it. I would recommend committing with equal dedication to your 'off-duty' hours, to allow yourself to enjoy your well-earned leisure and maintain a balance, so your loved ones don't suffer.

Take action
- Celebrations are a form of milestone to check how far you have come and where you are in achieving your goals. Take time out to enjoy your successes and to take stock of the position you have reached in the marketplace.
- Although it's not my style to do so, there is a case in some industries, such as the media, for networking socially with influential colleagues. You will gain recognition and have access to new business opportunities if you know the right people.

Fast forward to the future

It's very important for me to recognize that I am now in my late fifties and what that means for my businesses. One of the things I like about myself is that **I realize my weaknesses**, and one of my weaknesses is that as I get older I have to learn to understand that there is a different commercial world out there – entirely different from the one I grew up in. It's no longer a world where one trader talks to another and strikes a deal, where you can generally rely upon a level of honesty and integrity whatever the sector. It's now a cut-throat world driven by a new wave of young business people who have been brought up in a different way – a way that doesn't automatically include loyalty as part and parcel of the business equation.

When I talk about loyalties changing, I don't mean company loyalty. I mean in respect to buying and selling, customer and supplier relationship loyalty; 'handshake' loyalty. There's no point me arguing and screaming or shouting about it, wanting things done in the old-fashioned way. **I have to adapt**. Of course it's very hard for me to adapt because old habits die hard, they really do; but I have to accept that **the business world is changing** and to learn to understand it in its new guise.

I do this by recognising the need to employ young people, young lieutenants who are thinking the same way as others in the marketplace, who are brought up in this new world and know how to operate in it.

Be the best
Desire to achieve your full potential
There is no point in being half-hearted about doing something. Putting in long working hours at half-speed is a waste of time and will lead to reduced

> 'Belief in what you're doing
> is important – and making a
> contribution is important to me.'
>
> **AN APPRENTICE**

ability to perform effectively and poor results. My personal goal is not to be better than everyone else – that smacks of a superior attitude that I would not respect in anyone. **My personal goal is to be true to myself** and to become the best that I personally can be.

A desire to be the best was a trait shared by most taking part in *The Apprentice*. The majority showed a tremendous level of **commitment** and were determined to show themselves at their best. That's what makes a lasting impression on clients and customers – and potential employers!

Take action
- Only you will know what your goals are and how you see yourself in life. These areas are closely linked to self-belief and self-discipline (see pages 74 and 90). Much of what you learn and how you react in business will teach you about who you are, but as well as knowing your strengths try to observe consciously and improve those aspects of your nature that are your weak points. Your business is an expression of yourself, and it will benefit as a result.

Putting something back
Contributing to the bigger life picture
I do charity work not because I want people to say what a good fellow I am, but because I believe **it's the right thing to do**. There is nothing more satisfying than meeting an unemployed youngster from, say, Glasgow and hearing him say that my speech has inspired him, that he is going to go out there, get stuck in and have a go.

For the last few years I've felt that **I want to put something back** into the community. I really get a buzz out of helping someone else take the route

I've taken and do exactly what I've done. There's nothing wrong, of course, with inheriting wealth or enhancing it and making it better. Lord Kalms, then Stanley Kalms of Dixons, was a classic example. He worked in his father's business and succeeded in taking it from one level to another – a great achievement. I look back to 'the old days' and reflect upon the place where I started, and I think about the people I grew up with and the community I knew, and I want to put something back. I think it's very important to put something back; it cannot just be one-way traffic.

I am a massive taxpayer in this country. Just to wind me up, I keep pictures on the wall in my office of cheques written to the Inland Revenue – £48 million in one year, £28 million in another. Some people would go to extreme lengths for the right not to pay that money. Many actually leave the country to avoid paying such amounts of tax. But you know, as far as I'm concerned, I live in this country, I like Britain, I like British people, I have to live by the rules. I have learnt to take a very pragmatic view. I don't look at the £48 million tax I paid – I look at the other £120-odd million that I was allowed to keep.

I'm very much a British person, and I like to support where I've come from. The fact that I earn a significant amount of **money gives me choice** and allows me to make charitable contributions that will make a difference to a community. My work for charity has nothing to do with my businesses. My businesses are commercial ventures. The money that I invest in charitable concerns is strictly personal.

Belief in what they were doing and a desire to make a difference in life was common to all the Apprentices. They weren't just involved for financial reward – that was clear.

Take action

- Success and financial independence bring responsibilities. You have made it at the expense of and with the help of others, so make sure you are not assuming the glory is all yours. Give credit where it's due.
- We all have roots and we each owe our successes in part to others we have encountered during the course of our lives. Have you thought about who you should be grateful to and have you given them due gratitude and recognition?
- Putting something back is related to the idea of work–life balance. Take stock of the way you use your time. If you are always 'too busy' to help others, you have got something badly wrong.
- Self-regard comes from giving to others. It is a lesson that we often learn too late in life, so I am passing the information on now, for free.
- I've said it before in a different context: no man is an island. As a kid did you ever give yourself an extended address in your exercise book? My House, The Street, Hackney, London, England, UK, Europe, The World, The Universe? We are each a part of something bigger than ourselves, and it's important to remember that.

Keep learning

To succeed you need to be hungry for new experiences

Growing up through my own business life I must have had mentors, but don't ask me who they were because I don't know. There would have been, throughout my life, people that I used to pick up snippets of information from. I would have absorbed it, taken it in like a sponge, not realizing at the time that I was learning from someone that I admired, and then later overtook. I've done that, and I've seen it happen many times.

I've reflected back in my life and can think of lots of people who I once looked up to as business idols because they were running a business that had made £100,000 turnover in a year; but then, three years later, I'm running a company with a £3 million turnover and I've overtaken them. That is the way of the world, and there is another generation up and coming that will do the same to me. So **there are lots of people I've learnt from**, and I hope there are many that have learnt from me. That's what success is all about – learning.

For the rest of my life I'll learn, as will others who've reached the top. That's why many organizations and companies have as their figurehead a man or woman of 60+ years. Not because he or she is an expert in a particular company's business or products, but because they know, they've seen everything, they've tried everything. They've listened to every salesman, every marketing person, every engineer, every production planner. They've absorbed the valleys and mountains of industrial disaster, financial collapse, economic downturn, political change. They've seen it all, so they know what *not* to do. You can't replace that. You can't get that degree of experience and knowledge out of a can, and you can't buy it in a book. You can't put, corny though it may seem, an old head on young shoulders; the young head is going to have to learn the hard way. So I'm learning all the time – and I am hoping that the Apprentices will too.

Take action
- Keep an open mind and recognize that every day you are learning something new and that lessons can come from both the most obvious and the most unlikely sources.
- If you think you already know it all, you are likely to fail in business, so if that is your instinct, take stock and start listening.

You might be surprised by what you learn.
• Continuing to learn is one of the most important keys to succeeding in business. The business world is constantly changing, so make sure you are willing to learn new skills or you will get stuck in an outdated rut.

TESTING THE APPRENTICES

PART 2

4

THE 12-WEEK JOB INTERVIEW

Some people might have expected that applying to be my Apprentice would involve the interview from hell. Well, I wouldn't describe it as hell, but it was demanding, and it ensured that the person who got through the process would be good – bloody good!

gave the Apprentices 12 tasks to perform. These were designed to be tough. They were designed to push personal boundaries and to put each candidate under pressure. They were designed to bring out the true personality of each individual. They were also intended to be realistic – in scope, in time-frame and in results.

The rules of the game

Even in business, where every company is seeking new ways of operating, there are basic rules of engagement. It is important to be trusted, to be seen as someone who is straight – who delivers what's been promised on the date arranged and at the price agreed. To help our ambitious young contenders to stay on the straight and narrow – and to ensure that the odds remained even across the pack – we drew up the following rules.

Rules of all tasks

- You must not misrepresent yourself or make any false claims during the course of the tasks.
- You may not receive assistance from anyone familiar to you who is not part of the task.
- You may not mention *The Apprentice* or Sir Alan Sugar while researching.

The Apprentice was not an ordinary job interview, but the criteria for selection were the same. I wanted to see who could make brave decisions and have the courage of their convictions; who could come up with creative and flexible solutions; who was likely to pass the buck or cave in under pressure. I wanted to know which Apprentices I could rely upon for personal loyalty in a crisis, and which were more interested in personal gain than the success of the group. And I wanted to know who I could work with: who

> 'If you lot go to London on your day off and decide to pop
> into Madame Tussauds, make sure you keep moving
> – as people won't know who the real dummies are!'
>
> **SIR ALAN**

I would want to see at the helm of one of my companies, representing me, my family, my staff and all that the Amstrad organization stands for.

What does it take to get to the top?

It depends upon where you envisage 'the top' to be. Trying to leap from A to Z in one motion will not work. Dividing your challenge into business targets and progressing in conscious steps can take you to Jupiter and back if that's where you want to go.

As for academic qualifications – although they are an increasingly important currency in getting your first job, they are not a true indicator of longer term commercial success. The lists below show how millionaires of different academic backgrounds ranked, in order of importance, the qualities shared by all millionaires.

Non-academic at school	Academic at school
Being honest	**Having a high IQ**
Getting on with people	Being honest
Self-discipline	Having a supportive spouse
Having a supportive spouse	Having a passion for your work
Having a passion for your work	**Getting on with people**
Seeing business opportunities that others don't see	Seeing business opportunities that others don't see
Being well organized	Being a specialist
Finding a profitable market niche	Being well organized
Ignoring unconstructive criticism	Ignoring unconstructive criticism
Having mentors	Having mentors
Being a specialist	**Self-discipline**
Having a high IQ	Finding a profitable market niche

Adapted from information in *The Millionaire Mind*, Thomas J. Stanley (Bantam Books, 2000)

Apart from the fact that those with a high IQ seem to think less of the need for self-discipline than those who are non-academic, and those who are thought of as non-academic seem to reject the importance of IQ altogether, there are a lot of similarities between the two columns. Perhaps the non-academics put 'getting on with people' higher up the list because they don't have a piece of paper or the right background to open doors for them. Similarly, they need to be self-disciplined because they have more to prove. These things apart, there is really very little difference between the two lists.

The Apprentices offered an interesting cross-section of skills and abilities, and came from an interesting variety of backgrounds. The 12-week interview process, with barely any access to friends and families, was to be a personal journey for everyone involved in the project.

This section of the book has been written so that you, the reader, can easily adapt the tasks the Apprentices undertook by considering the issues discussed and questions raised in the context of your own business circumstances. You will all have been in situations where you have had to carry out some or all of the tasks our candidates were taking part in, so use your own experiences of trying to sell, buy, negotiate, or start a business project, to learn more about your suitability to succeed as an entrepreneur.

Basic business skills

The following skills apply to you, to me, and to anyone who is in business. The best advice I can give you, whether you are starting your own business or have aspirations to progress within your current career environment, is that you need to **start progressing from where you are, not from where you'd like to be, or where you think you are.**

Be realistic about your level of experience, your level of working capital and your abilities. Don't try to pretend you are someone you are not, but take stock and assess whether you have the skills to succeed. Where there are gaps in your knowledge or experience, **find advisors or business partners** to help you achieve your aim – but make sure they are people that you know (if only through recommendation) and that you can trust.

To be successful in business you need to:
- Understand your strengths and weaknesses.
- Understand the value of time.
- Utilize what you are best at, and focus the optimum amount of your time on doing it.
- Employ or pay other people to do the rest of the tasks.

Commercially you need to:
- Focus on the bottom line.
- Focus on achieving your target, e.g. profit or sales volume or numbers of some kind.
- By whatever efforts are necessary, make sure you plan the task successfully.
- Be well organized.
- Be able to grasp a situation quickly.
- Be prepared for disaster.
- Be flexible/adaptable.
- Realize that timing is crucial – ensure you're entering and leaving the marketplace at the right time.
- Build in regular 'reality checks' to make sure you're still focused, profitable and backing the right product.

Each of the tasks set for the Apprentices was designed to test core business skills that are relevant to every business, whether you are in a service industry, in manufacturing, in commercial or retail sales, and increasingly in the public sector as well. The general comments and guidelines given here are intended to inspire you, to give you food for thought whatever your walk of life. Whether you are a young entrepreneur, a mature business person, or someone who has had self-employment thrust upon you and you're hungry to launch your own venture, I hope that these tasks will enable you to reconsider your own approach to business and to learn and adapt as necessary. The tasks were designed to assess the following business skills:

Selling – understanding your market
Product design – the gambling instinct
Buying – how to win at negotiating
Retail management – stock selection and sales skills
Closing the deal – focusing on the bottom line
Advertising – marketing and branding
People management – charity fund-raising
Margins – controlling your costs
Direct selling – the challenge of selling face to face
Sales presentation – an electronic trip to the market
Interviewing – interviews and how to survive them
Event management – the art of planning and leadership

Watch your mouth

There's one lesson that I had to teach the Apprentices quite early on. An organization has room for only one Big Mouth, and you'd better be sure that that big mouth is the person at the top.

If the person at the top loses his or her cool, the person on the receiving end will probably accept it – albeit unwillingly. If the company's lieutenants try it, it doesn't work. So if you have a problem, don't lose your temper, make sure you refer the issue upwards. You can be sure that it will eventually get to the top anyway, so you might as well deal with the problem yourself and nip it in the bud.

Remember – business isn't about you: it's about making a profit for the good of the company as a whole. Anything you do to jeopardize that jeopardizes the fortunes of others in the company as well.

Week 1: Selling
Understanding your market

I am often asked how I decide which ideas are runners or winners and which to walk away from. The truth is that much of the decision-making comes down to experience. We all make mistakes and learn from our mistakes along the way. But the most important business lessons are:

- To truly **understand what the end consumer wants**.
- To **ensure that the product is suitable** for the market
  – by that I mean in price, in quality and in volume.
- To establish that the product has enough **potential to be life-changing**.

Every product needs to be innovative and offer something new.

The reason **I have no interest in 'me too' products** is because **if they're already on the market, there's no certainty that anyone will buy them from *us***. An entrepreneur concentrates on keeping ahead of the game.

Getting the market to change
Great business success stories are all about getting the market to change. I'll give you a classic example: Amstrad didn't invent computers, but we recognized that we could make them at a very, very low price. More than that, we made computers that performed in the same way as other computers. In that way we expanded the home computer market.

Before the advent of our low-priced IBM-compatible computer, computers were used only by business people and accountants and were very expensive items. Amstrad changed the world – quite literally, we changed it. We brought out the IBM-compatible computer for £400. No one could believe the price. The other computers on the market were all priced in the region of £4000. We changed the market forever because we were producing a life-changing product. We had a similar success when we brought out word processors at a cheap price while everyone was still using typewriters. The mobile phone is another example of a product that has changed everybody's lives. We're not taking the credit for that, obviously, but as we develop new products in this marketplace we hope that they will expand the market horizons too.

I confine ideas for expansion to things I am genuinely interested in, and ensure that I have rock-solid customer knowledge – of what they will buy and what they want – before I begin the expensive process of product development.

The art of selling

Selling is really a simpler task than buying, provided of course that you have the right product to sell. At the end of the day the right product will sell itself for you. Once your market knows it's out there, they will seek it out.

Of course, you can't sell something to people that they don't want. You can try – and people do try – but if you do, you don't end up with customers for very long, and you definitely won't get a repeat purchase.

In our industry we're always talking to the same customers. We don't have anyone else to sell to! So we need to take responsibility for maintaining our side of the relationship. There's a balance to be achieved between not lumbering them with too much stock while getting them to buy as much as possible.

In the electronics market it's a false economy to oversupply customers beyond the level that the market will take because it ties up the retailers' cash, it takes up their shelf space and it leaves a bad taste. They will remember it as a bad deal.

The same may not be true in other industries, however. If you were a jeweller in the West End of London, you might decide to offload stock in bulk because the customer could be a transient buyer you are unlikely to see again. That might be an instance where heavy, forceful salesmanship could be used to great effect because you're not anticipating repeat business. However, a provincial jeweller might be less likely to take such a tough stance because he relies upon selling to a smaller nucleus of people and wants to build a reputation of good service and good value.

The fashion industry offers a great example of a sector where **high-pressure selling** can bring results but turn people off longer term. Most people will, at some time, have gone into a clothing store where a retailer is putting on the pressure to such a degree that you end up buying something that you don't want, just to get them off your back. But one thing's for sure, you won't go back there again. You'll never go back, even if you see something nice, because you don't want to be intimidated into buying something else that you don't want.

Repeat business

Repeat business is vitally important for the profit and longevity of a company. You must not risk alienating your customers if you want them to come back again. An intuitive understanding of **body language** is crucial. You've got to be tough but reasonable, and you've got to understand who you're selling to.

Planning your approach

Selling a product is all about recognizing your objective, then planning and acting to achieve the right result. There are no statistics to help with the sale of a new or innovative product, so you have to be ready to impress customers in other ways – through investment.

What attracts customers?
- Features.
- Price – it needs to fall within their range of disposable income.
- Facilities.
- Newness/originality.
- The 'everyone should have one' factor.
- It should be an easy buy, a worry-free purchase.

What attracts traders?
Traders don't tend to be innovators. They want:
- A safe bet, an easy sell – preferably with a track record.
- Statistics to show them how, when and where to sell.
- Investment to help them market and sell the product.

Spotting a niche

One of the characteristics of successful business people is their ability to spot a niche opportunity in the marketplace and to grow it into something bigger. My own break into manufacturing was through recognition of a very small market for an accessory (a polythene hi-fi cover) that manufacturers were then producing using a process that was rather expensive – simply because they didn't wish to invest in machinery that would enable them to be made far more cheaply. I recognized that I could make them at a much lower price if I made an investment in the right machine.

It was quite a gamble at the time because the market wasn't huge, but it was growing. I could make the covers at about a quarter of the price that the other people could make them for. The clever thing was that I could sell them at a slightly lower price but in the same price range as the others were selling them. I had a massive margin, whereas they didn't have much of a margin at all.

The sales personality

No matter how well organized you are and no matter how many features your new niche product has, you will only make a success of your business if you can sell. The salesperson needs to have **personality, drive, a competitive edge, focus and the ability to close the deal**. It was these characteristics that I was looking for in setting the first task for the Apprentices.

'I could go out and sell £10 notes for £9 each
all day long with no problem I can tell you!
But even I wouldn't make a profit.'

SIR ALAN

Task 1: The hard sell

GOAL: To sell on the streets of London
CHALLENGE: To buy cheap, sell high and maximize profit

Rules and regulations
- The teams were given £400 seed money to start their own one-day business.
- They could use only seed money for the specific task or money earned directly from the specific task.
- They had to buy stock and sundries for their business. This involved negotiating the best deal possible on whatever they thought would sell.
- Teams could sell only in specified locations.
- The teams had a few hours to sell as much as they could.
- They could not remain in the same place for more than two hours.
- They could sell anywhere on the pavement and they could try to sell to restaurants/offices.
- Teams could not try to sell their product within 30 metres of an existing stall or seller selling the same product.
- The teams had to reconcile their receipts and sales.
- The winner was the team that made the most profit.

Skills tested
- Being street smart.
- Buying stock at the cheapest price possible.
- Selling at the optimum price.
- Selecting a location where they would be able to close sales effectively.

- Recognizing whether or not the strategy was working and to adjust a) location or b) price, as necessary.
- Not dropping the price too early in the day.
- Selling in large numbers by working hard and closing sales.

Being street smart

In this context being street smart meant knowing London well enough to choose locations where there would be enough passing traffic to allow the possibility of bulk sales, and where the type of customer was likely to part company with hard-earned cash.

Location, location, location

Flexibility in choosing both location and price are necessary, depending upon the type of product for sale and whether or not it is perishable. There was quite a bit of debate among our candidates on this point. Some knew their locations better than others.

Right customer, right price

Perishable products command different prices depending on the time of day and location. Punters at the Wimbledon tennis championships, for example, will buy strawberries at a high price at any time of day, no matter what size the portion (although quality of presentation is an expectation). However, people buying the same quality of strawberries from a street market will pay less towards the end of the day because the market-traders have to drop the price if they want to clear their stalls and avoid wastage. And goods like flowers have an even greater range of prices, places and customers.

How would our teams get on? Not all our Apprentices saw eye to eye on pricing. Crucially, this was also a test of team-building, leadership, followership and honesty. Once the strategy was in place, would all team members agree with it and follow it? This was the first task, so it was going to be a challenge for the leaders to rein in all the egos. As one candidate said, 'It was difficult: there were 14 natural leaders and no natural followers. Everyone was shouting over everyone else. It was chaos!' Would they manage to get down to business and how would the winning team succeed?

Danger point: Disorganization

It was important in these tasks that everyone pull together, and I was watching out for that just as I would do in my normal business life. It's vital for company survival that everyone stays alert and understands what is going on. There was a danger that if the team leader did not hold things together, the others would head off in different directions.

Business lesson: Respecting authority

Disorganization occurs when the team leader is not being clear enough and is allowing more than one star to emerge from the group. Not everyone can be the star of the show. In a competitive situation individuals may feel they have to shine as a star in order to win the overall prize. If they operate in a way that is at the expense of their colleagues they fail.

Week 2: Product design
The gambling instinct

People in the electronics industry would say, 'Sugar is a gambler. He gambles on products, he gambles on new concepts and he might win six, lose four.' I would agree with them. **You have to be a big gambler to win at this game.**

But then again, it's not recklessness. It's a case of knowing that the only way to continue to exist is to have something different from giant competitors. And in order to have something different, you've got to gamble to some extent whether something's going to be right or not. I'm certainly not always right. But to offset the risks of gambling on products and development ideas, I've got a huge property portfolio, which is really very safe and boring in comparison.

Calculated risk

Fifteen years ago I woke up to the fact that I had plenty of money, and a family and other commitments – and yet I was a gambler. I thought to myself, 'You've seen how quick you can make it – and you've also seen how quickly you can lose it.' I mean, one year we lost £70 million. So I decided that I was going to take part of my personal wealth and put it into property. Property is a completely different business. It bores me really. I'm not particularly interested in it at all. It's there to build safe foundations for my family, or for whoever is around me, and for other commitments that I care to make.

Having said that, some people in the property business will say, 'He says it's boring, but he still seems to have some aptitude for the business. He seems to buy the right properties. He doesn't get lumbered with anything – they all seem to be in the right position, they all seem to be let and he doesn't sell anything. He just keeps buying and he doesn't sell anything. So he's not that much of a dummy.'

Well, I'm not saying that because I find it boring I have to be stupid! But I've balanced out the commercial side of my life. I've got businesses like Amstrad and Viglen, the computer operations, where I'm constantly gambling with products and innovation, and on the other side I have become more stable. I've hedged my bets, if you understand me.

It's common knowledge that I am suspicious of people who owe their position to privilege rather than hard work, and I have no respect for those who are simply 'working the system'. That doesn't mean I am against people who come from a different background from my own. That would be ridiculous. What concerns me is when people who don't care about the big picture, who are only interested in immediate personal gain, start to hold positions of influence in business, then the whole marketplace suffers.

How does a company go about designing a new product?

In many instances, especially in the electronics industry, each product evolves from the one that has gone before it. You have to remember that the company concerned is already operating within a defined industry niche, so the company profile and the company's products will already be well defined.

Changes in the style and fashion of the product **are dictated by the needs of the market**. Before spending a vast amount of money on market research, a company is well advised to glean feedback from its sales and marketing teams. What do they want to sell? What pricing level is required? What features are desired?

A study has to be undertaken before spending money on design or development:

- Can it be made at the preferred price?
- Is the technology able to do it?
- Will it be obsolete by the time it comes out?

If the answers are, 'Yes, we can do it in time' and 'Yes, we can meet our pricing criteria', the product is handed over to the designers for tooling a prototype.

All companies need to **listen first** to what their sales people say before employing market researchers. Salespeople can give you feedback as to why something is not selling and why something else would sell better. Although in my experience 90 per cent of feedback can be disregarded, 10 per cent is pure gold and something that you can build on.

The next best thing

In our business everything is very much feature-driven. In that way the electronics industry is very like the toy business in that flashing lights and clever gizmos are very appealing to certain customers. In other ways selling computers is more about providing sheer power. There is no point in telling a retailer that no one will ever fill up a 300-gigabyte drive, for example, and that their customers really don't need these. The retailer doesn't care. **If the market wants one, the market has to have one.** We're constantly chasing our tails to provide the next best thing.

Marketing and technical people need to be aware of how fast technology is moving, and be ready to raise the alert, and even to pull the plug or, if necessary, change the direction of a particular product's development halfway through. But it is very important to decide what the main features are going to be.

The importance of market knowledge

Of course, within the context of the television series, the time constraints were such that our Apprentices would be challenged to learn on their feet very quickly in each task, and make maximum use of their expert advisers. When faced with product design for the first time, would they make wise decisions and take the advice of the right people?

The key factors for the team leaders would be to achieve consensus among the team members, to acquire accurate market knowledge and feedback from reputable sources, and to brief their designers effectively and in a focused manner. They needed to ensure that the final product would be profitable at less than £10 and would deliver something genuinely new and exciting to the marketplace – quite a challenge.

This was a favourite task among a few of our candidates, especially those who had never spent time in a design studio before. Perhaps inevitably, given the number of people involved, there was difficulty in reaching consensus on the design. Those with more assertive personalities were definitely starting to take the lead.

Innovation versus product enhancements

Very rarely is product design a brand new thing. It's an enhancement of something that has gone before, that the company already has within its existing range of products, or that its competitors have.

If you look at car design, for example, only once every 10 years will the basic body shape change. One manufacturer does it, then all the others follow suit. It is often external factors that dictate a change: for instance, the fuel crisis in the late 1970s saw car design change radically under the Carter administration in the United States. The large gas-guzzlers of the past were gradually surpassed by smaller, more aerodynamic vehicles that offered more speed with less resistance, and therefore greater fuel economy.

The designers' job is to make the product look good once all the basic criteria have been decided upon.

Product design in action

I'm **observing the market** all the time, and **seeing opportunities** arising all the time. At Amstrad three or four of us will generally sit down and brainstorm a new idea. We don't have official meetings. We send each other press cuttings, snippets of ideas and information. Each of these triggers a thought that gradually builds into the whole.

I also have a network of contacts in consultancies who are looking at other niches. We **exchange ideas** about what could be good for this or that. I have people who contact me and say, 'This could be right up your alley … this is just the thing for you.'

I'd like to think that an early Amstrad product could be recognized for its uniqueness in 100 years' time – an electronic antique if you like!

'Never rely solely upon market research from your consumers; there is a danger they will tell you what they think you want to hear.'

SIR ALAN

Task 2: Designing a product

GOAL: To create a product from scratch
CHALLENGE: To use brainstorming skills, focus groups and consultancies to judge an unknown market

Rules and regulations
- The teams had to design a prototype for an original product without using copyrighted images or registered characters
- The finished item had to retail at £10 or less.
- The teams had to make a prototype.
- Each team had £300 to buy research materials.
- They had to pitch their concepts and explain why they would be 'the next big thing'.
- A product-expert panel would tell me which team, in its opinion, was the winner.

Skills tested
- Evaluating a brief.
- Working with experts.
- Extracting information from data.
- Imagination in coming up with new ideas.
- Pitching an idea.

Evaluating a brief
When evaluating a brief, several critical areas have to be considered: the originality of the idea, the amount of time available, the costs and logistics of developing it, and the price at which it will sell. In most cases a feasibility study will be required, so make sure you approach qualified people for help.

Working with experts

It is important to **keep an open mind.** As a manufacturer, you can never trust yourself to be the only market expert. You need the cooperation and interest of those who are out there selling the products. In the case of our Apprentices, who had no knowledge of the market sector at all, it would be important for them to consult those who had industry experience. Note: it is important to remember that you are **building professional relationships** at all times and to treat people with the respect they deserve.

Extracting information from data

Data should be approached with caution and should not be looked at in isolation from discussion with experts or other market research. It can give an indication of trends, and may reveal whether you are backing an idea that has had its day, but if you are launching a groundbreaking and brand new idea, you won't find an exact match for your product.

Imagination in coming up with new ideas

Received wisdom has it that there is no such thing as a new idea. In many ways that is true. Even the most advanced technological breakthroughs tend to be enhancing a previous product or service. The key then is to ensure that your idea has 'legs' in its current manifestation. Test it out on a focus group, make sure that it will be genuinely profitable, and **don't over-produce** until you have some committed buyers on board.

Pitching a final idea

In order to **sell your idea** you need enthusiasm and clarity. Your audience needs to be able to understand clearly what you are offering, both in the context of previous market successes and also in terms of originality, value for money and new features.

Our Apprentices had a few challenges with this task. They weren't short of ideas, but would they choose the right one to put into development? Could it be developed economically? Would they assess the market requirements accurately? The same questions apply no matter which market sector you are entering.

Danger point: Health and safety regulations

We live in increasingly litigious times, and manufacturers are increasingly constrained by health and safety considerations. Products need to be made with materials that are non-toxic; components need to be of a size that ensures small children won't swallow or choke on them; polythene bags need to be perforated to avoid suffocation … and, on top of all that, you need to create something that will have appeal.

Business lesson: Decision-making

It's easy to waste a lot of time on the wrong idea. Listening and a flexible approach are vital to success. It is generally very unwise to insist on a course of action that everyone else is fervently against. It's more usual that 10 say 'A' and three say 'B', or the decision is split 50:50.

A leader acts as a sponge really, absorbing information from all quarters. People often think that I don't listen, but I do. I don't miss a trick. I listen to every single thing that is said and I can quote it back when necessary. The art of strong leadership is having the ability to fully appraise a situation and to be decisive. Making the ultimate decision – that's the bottom line. That said, I can't just define a complete strategy for a product and tell people to go away and get on with it.

Week 3: Buying
How to win at negotiating

When you negotiate, you need to **begin with a clear objective** in mind. You need to know what you're trying to achieve before you pick up the phone, before you arrange the meeting, before you open your mouth.

Your **style of negotiation depends on who you're dealing with** – whether you're **buying** or whether you're **selling**. Within Amstrad we have a very stable base of suppliers. They don't change a lot because they are mainly component suppliers. So how do we negotiate when our supplier base is relatively static? What we do is set up a proposition. We recognize what motivates the suppliers – what rings their bells.

What normally rings their bells is the anticipation of a big order – and in our case the consistency or the longevity of the order. Doing business with us means that suppliers are not just earning revenue today – they are going to get a consistent amount of business over an extended period of time, and can plan for that revenue stream as part of their annual turnover. **Big-volume orders** over a long period of time are very attractive to suppliers. We're not just going to turn up tomorrow, buy a few items and never be seen again, so there's a strong proposition around which to build a good negotiation.

Our aim is to negotiate the lowest unit cost possible. Their aim is to get the highest margin on their product.

The usual thing for the purchaser to do when negotiating is to compare what prices the suppliers' competitors are charging for a similar product and to construct an argument that states: while you wish to remain loyal to an existing supplier, you can't ignore what is available in the rest of the world. Of course our Apprentices would not have the advantage of building long-term relationships – but I was watching for how they would begin the relationship and manage the discussion in the first place.

The importance of supplier relationships

My staff are not the type of people who chop and change suppliers just for the sake of it, or for the short-term gain of a few pennies. If you're thinking of changing suppliers, it's important to give your **long-term business partners** the opportunity of competing. But first of all you have to weigh up in your own mind whether it's a false economy to jump from one supplier to another. On many occasions, in the long run it will actually cost you more (but perhaps you don't let that be known to the supplier when you're negotiating!).

I've always found that suppliers have got on very well with us over the years. They may not get the right impression initially because we're tough negotiators and we have **high expectations.** In the long haul, however, if you speak to our suppliers, you'll find that they love us – and the reason is because they get it straight. They don't get any false promises – and if a product is successful, they get **repeat orders.**

There are, of course, occasions when you might want to wind down some of the supplier commitments you have made. You might be disappointed with their quality, their pricing, their speed of delivery – or you might have found a better supplier elsewhere. In these instances I've always found that **honesty is the best policy**. Go and see your supplier, tell them your dilemma, tell them the truth of the matter rather than trying to wriggle out with some excuse or by trying to construct an argument that puts the blame on them. They will appreciate your honesty, and may even be able to come up with a solution to the problem or some inside information about their competitor. It is an approach that works – it's always worked for me. Our Apprentices needed to learn to speak to business partners with respect in order to achieve an outcome that was mutually beneficial.

A deal is a deal

When we do a deal, it might be a tough deal, and our suppliers might wonder sometimes whether they have a genuinely good deal, but the one thing they can guarantee is that we're going to take the merchandise – and that is not always guaranteed in this business. I don't like people who renege on me, and we certainly don't have a culture of reneging on things that we agree to.

We've made quite a few mistakes in doing deals on certain things, no question about it. Sometimes you have to pay for your mistakes, you have to take the goods and the commitment is paid off. Some of my staff, especially the younger ones, have taken a long time to grasp the logic of this approach. They can't understand sometimes that if things are bad, and you've made a commitment to a supplier, why you continue to take their goods, why you continue to ship them. They've got to understand that you've made a **moral commitment**. You've made a deal and you just can't ignore that.

As far as I'm concerned, if we've placed an order, I've written a cheque. To my mind, backtracking is the same as bouncing a cheque. What's done is done. I'll go along and talk to the supplier if things are not right, but **I won't use tricky means** to avoid taking the merchandise.

When things go wrong

Losing out on a deal can feel as if luck has gone against you, but usually, if you look at the situation honestly, you will see where improvements could have been made. Perhaps you were trying to get a good price from a vendor who was not a decision-maker and was therefore unable to negotiate or authorize a discount; perhaps you were trying to buy from the wrong kind of vendor. It is important to get as far back in the supply chain as possible, namely, to the manufacturer, the distributor or the wholesaler, rather than the retailer, in order to negotiate the lowest feasible price.

The reasons for failure will influence future decision-making. **Excuses for failure are never acceptable.** Excuses are about ducking responsibility and get you nowhere. So make sure when you are taking stock that you find a way of appraising the situation honestly and take steps to **improve your methodology** in future. This was a message that I had to relay to the teams on *The Apprentice* on more than one occasion!

'You've given me so many excuses you remind me of my football managers. In fact, you've taught them a few tricks!'

SIR ALAN

Task 3: Discount buying

GOAL: To buy to order from a list of unrelated products
CHALLENGE: Negotiating the best deal for specified merchandise

Rules and regulations
- The teams had to use their negotiation skills to purchase 10 items for as low a price as possible.
- They received seed money of £750.
- They had to turn in the purchased items, receipts and remaining money and an account of their expenses.
- The team that spent the least was the winner.

Skills tested
- Drawing up a purchasing strategy.
- Delegating to the team.
- Talking the vendor down to the cheapest price.

Drawing up a purchasing strategy
Without a strategy, chaos will rule – especially if a number of different purchases need to be made quite fast and in different locations. To purchase effectively requires research: the buyer needs to know what the market prices are and where to get the cheapest stock from, so a good sense of location and timing are critical. Your buyer or buyers need to be in the right place at the right time in order to achieve the optimum deal.

Delegating to the team
The art of delegation is not to give everyone impressive job titles, then leave them to get on with the task. Instead, the team leaders should ensure that they are playing to everyone's strengths. They need to clarify individual roles and make sure they know what their priorities are. It is then

essential to stay in regular contact to **keep the teams motivated** and on track. Only by doing these things can the project be delivered successfully, on time and to budget.

Talking down the price
A vendor will reduce his price only if it brings him a specific benefit. His aim is to make a profit, and he needs to see the advantage of selling at lower than the market price. A good negotiator will be well prepared, will have researched the subject and will be able to set out the advantages of the sale to the vendor.

Danger point: Insubordination

If you are put in a team reporting to a team leader, it is up to you to get on with delivering the job in hand – and it is up to the team leader to motivate you and other members of the team to deliver. But sometimes you have a person in the team who rebels just for the sake of rebelling. It doesn't matter how much you try to motivate or encourage that person, he or she becomes a semi-saboteur.

The business lesson: Prioritizing

The leader has to stay focused on the task in hand and tackle the problem of rebellion at a later point. There's no point in trying to deal with it on the job because you'll waste valuable time. After the event you can make your feelings very clear, and unless the person has pretty good reasons for their behaviour, you don't need that kind of individual in your team.

In the tasks set for the Apprentices, I was looking for cooperation. It was the Apprentices' responsibility to use their best endeavours to follow the leader and deliver to the brief.

Week 4: Retail management
Stock selection and sales skills

I haven't been a retailer myself since my earliest days. I wasn't bad at selling, but dealing with the public face to face presents a different kind of challenge to selling business to business. My knowledge of the area comes from my viewpoint as a manufacturer.

At Amstrad we recently launched our E3 videophone. A lot of work and effort has gone into the phone, and a lot of learning from past mistakes. Now we are having to invest in teaching our retailers how to sell the product. We have taken care not to over-produce because the technology changes so fast and suppliers have fixed orders. It's conceivable that if it takes off very fast that we might run out – but I'd rather run out than have too many in stock. We'll get a feeling as it starts to sell of how quickly it's being bought by the public. For now, I will wait and see whether our E3 brainstorming: to add a coloured screen, make it a videophone, and to add loads more features, is really going to capture the attention of the public. If it does then we hope to sell a lot; and if it captures the public's imagination then it will encourage us to think – what can we do next?

These days a manufacturer has to battle to get a retailer to take an untested innovative product. The battle normally results in the manufacturer having to let the retailer have stock on some kind of sale or return basis, do some advertising for them, get them in the stores, pay for their point-of-sale material – actually to do all the work for them!

This is quite different to the old retail sales model where the retailer and manufacturer made decisions in partnership. In the days when great entrepreneurs like Stanley Kalms (founder of Dixons) or Jack Cohen (founder of Tesco) were around, a manufacturer like me who was good at manufacturing, would speak to a retailer like them who was good at retailing and there was no need to have to convince anyone else – they saw it for themselves. They would want the new product straight away – sometimes the whole lot!

If I want an opinion these days I am unlikely to go to one of the high-street chains – instead I will go to a privately owned store: large or small, because I want to speak to a business person who owns the shop, who is operating at the front line; whose personal profit margin depends upon the stock-buying decisions that are made. Someone who touches the merchandise, feels it, is on the doorstep all the time – they know! You show him or her something and they can give you an honest answer straight away.

The key business lesson in retail management relates to the **choice and range of product**. This needs to be combined with careful attention to floor display and signage. As ever, **location is everything**. I was able to arrange for the candidates to experience their next task at one of the most extraordinary privately owned stores in the world. They would have access to some of the most talented and well-trained retail managers in London.

This was a high-calibre task for the Apprentices and a true test of business acumen and grit under pressure. The day was not without its drama. 'I've never been so undermined and demeaned in my life,' was the comment of one candidate, while one of the team leaders acknowledged that 'The task was a complete shambles first thing this morning'. Such high feeling – and all they had been asked to do was set up shop at the most prestigious retail outlet in the UK, if not the world! Focus and effective product selection were the keys to success. Which team would win, and how?

'A business lesson for all to learn is that fewer product lines can mean more money.'

SIR ALAN

Task 4: Running a department in a luxury store

GOAL: To run a given area of a department store
CHALLENGE: To choose a range of appropriate products at a price range that allowed a profit

A lot of behind-the-scenes energy had gone into arranging this location. It provided an opportunity for our Apprentices to really shine. They had free access to the store stocklist and were, in effect, departmental managers for the day. This was a genuine promotion.

Our Apprentices had a hectic timetable to fulfil before opening for business. They were in the hot seat. Their mettle was being tested. There would be no excuses for the losing team on this one.

Rules and regulations
- The teams had to select products to sell from a list of goods provided by the store. They could not sell anything that was not on the list.
- Each team had a seed fund of £600 to spend as it saw fit. All spending on the task days had to be drawn from this fund.
- The teams had to abide by the store's trading rules at all times.
- The store kept track of what had been sold. The team with the highest turnover was the winner.

Skills tested
- Product selection.
- Delegation.
- Flexibility.
- Calmness under pressure.

Product selection

When I briefed the candidates I reminded them that they needed to look at making **high-volume sales.** This did not necessarily mean stocking up with low-priced goods. The major lesson for all involved was that less is often more: in this particular case, fewer product lines could well mean more money.

Delegation

This was a task that required **effective team playing**. There was a lot to juggle and the days were long. There was no space for slacking, raised voices or disrespectful behaviour. A team leader in this situation needs to remain calmly confident, upbeat and organized. There was definitely no room for complacency.

Flexibility

While strategy and planning are very important, having **contingency plans** is also essential. This means that if things don't go according to plan, survival techniques are still possible. Retail selling is full of surprises.

Calmness under pressure

Leaders need to **keep calm in order to inspire**. The teams needed to keep calm for the good of each other. People's ability to remain calm can often be measured by how they speak to third parties. Let's just say that some candidates were more diplomatic than others.

Danger point: Appropriate price range

This was a task operating within a tight time-frame. It was important that the teams chose the right goods at the right prices to attract the sector of the public likely to be drawn to the department.

Business lesson: Distinguishing luck from hard work

A lot of people say that business success is founded on luck, and of course there is an element of luck involved in certain deals and on certain days. If you are in the right place at the right time and something occurs that is completely unexpected and unplanned that you benefit from, then of course luck plays its part. But there is no such thing as luck in long-term business. There is just hard work, determination and knowing what your business is all about.

Luck was debated quite hard in one of the tasks as playing its part for one of the teams. It might be tempting to agree, but usually there are other factors at play that contribute to success, such as effective planning and choice of products, pricing, display and selling skills. Because contestants had some success, a lot of people termed it 'luck'.

Week 5: Closing the deal
Focusing on the bottom line

A specialist dealer may tell you that it is important to educate the customer in order to persuade them to buy. I think that is nonsense. There are broadly three types of customer:

- Those who will make an impulse purchase.
- Those who don't understand what to buy and need some guidance.
- Those who don't necessarily like what they are buying, but are already well informed.

In my view you can't talk someone into buying anything. What you need to do is sense whether you have someone sniffing at the bait. That is where the talent comes in. Watch your customer's body language, spot whether someone has a genuine interest, and set about closing the deal.

Being condescending and schmoozy won't wash anywhere, whether in the refined environment of the arts or out there on the high street. Trying to persuade someone what they ought to be buying is the wrong way to go about it.

Connoisseurs of every industry tend to be rather po-faced and want to be left alone to make their own decisions. If you can detect this kind of person, it is best just to wait and listen, and to be ready to answer questions. Hopefully, their first question will be 'How much?' If their response in non-committal or negative, it is time to find out what the obstacle is. It may be that the price needs to go down a bit in order to clinch the deal.

There are others who will buy because they want to buy, but just don't know whether something is good or not. You can exploit that by giving them some facts to help them make an informed decision.

How do you tell who the real buyers are? At a launch event it can be tricky for the inexperienced to tell the difference between a buyer and a 'hanger-on' because there are many people who will be attracted by the ambience and the champagne and canapés. The Apprentices were faced with this scenario and would have found the distinction hard. But a few good opening questions should indicate fairly quickly whether the guests are potential buyers or not: 'Are you here to buy this evening? What kind of product do you usually buy?'

My own belief is that **selling is an instinct** that relates to some form of knowledge, which is innate in you. It's a kind of in-built sensitive intelligence that helps you sense and understand; something you were born with and you can build on and learn to use through experience. I instinctively know, and I have always known, when I have someone on the hook. **I know when I've got a deal**, and when you find yourself in this situation you have to close the deal there and then. If there is an obstacle, you need to detect it straight away. What is the deal-breaker?

The last thing you should do is let the customer go away and think about it or talk about it. You want to **get a commitment**, so you just keep hammering away at the obstacles, either subtly or not so subtly, depending upon your customer. A business transaction can sometimes go on for days, so you have to learn to hold your nerve, not make that final call, otherwise you come across as too anxious.

What is instinct?

My belief is that instinct is related to some form of knowledge that is innate in you, something you were born with, but also something that you can build on, that you could learn through experience. It's a kind of **inbuilt sensitive intelligence** that helps you to see and understand things without being conscious of it. There were some amongst the Apprentices who had this skill and others who found it hard. It was satisfying to watch some candidates discover a skill they didn't know they had, and to watch others hone their ability in different business scenarios.

The silent close

In selling there is a tough device used, which is called 'the silent close'. Any salesperson these days who has been on a training course will know about it. In the silent close you stay silent in order to force the other person to talk. A **deliberate silence** may last only a few seconds, but it might feel as if it has gone on for hours.

A silent close is usually used after the point when you have proffered your best deal, and you're implying, 'I don't mean to be rude, but I'm going now – this is your last chance'. You only come to understand how to use silence in negotiating by using it.

In my industry there is no point in selling something to someone if they don't want it or need it. It is a principle that will hold broadly true for every other sector as well.

'If a person doesn't like something, it
doesn't matter if you give it to them for
nothing, they are still not going to want it!'

SIR ALAN

Task 5: The art challenge

GOAL: To pick one artist and sell their work
CHALLENGE: To assess popular choice over specialist choice

Rules and regulations
- Both teams visited the same list of artists then decided who they wanted to represent.
- If both teams chose the same artist, the artist decided who would represent him/her.
- The teams selected pieces by their chosen artist to display for sale.
- They worked with the artists to decide on prices.
- The teams had to sell as much artwork as possible.

Skills tested
- Understanding popular choice.
- Making a profitable decision.
- Trusting judgement.
- Credibility in a closed commercial world.
- Getting potential customers through the door.
- Optimizing the team's effectiveness.

Understanding popular choice
Art selection can be quite daunting. Taste in art is very personal, and opinions about artistic works are deeply subjective – yet, as **with all sales tasks, normal rules apply**. It's whether your buyers like the product that matters. Of course, it's easier to sell if you like it too.

Making a profitable decision

Do you select low-priced art and opt for high turnover, or do you aim for the high end of the marketplace and recognize that you have to sell for the long haul? Our teams considered both options. This assignment was a tough one.

Trusting judgement

Body language always plays a part in selling, but in the art arena it is especially important. How would the artists weigh up our teams and decide who they wanted to represent them? How would our salespeople decide who to approach, and what was the right length of time to wait to close a deal?

Credibility in a closed commercial world

Surprisingly, some of the salespeople who had shone the most brightly in earlier tasks found that their skills were not as effective in this new arena. One candidate in particular found marked differences between this style of selling and what they were used to: 'I couldn't go in for the kill very early, or close early.'

Getting potential customers through the door

How would you go about getting the art-buying public over your threshold? Suave determination and the promise of an exciting evening? Or would the hard sell be more effective? Once through the door, how do you ensure everyone is attended to and that no potential buyers slip away? It is definitely a team effort, and there needs to be clear communication and flexibility all round.

Optimizing the team's effectiveness

Deciding who would connect best with the purchasers and how best to keep the teams motivated if sales were slow – these were the challenges to be tackled. This task offered one of the most interesting examples of how to combine different styles of sales techniques and keep cool under pressure, and it assessed whether the Apprentices would stay focused on profit or get caught up with assessing artistic talent. It was good to see so many people putting into practice the lessons learnt previously.

Danger point: Working as a team

In some businesses, such as the jewellery trade, the clothing industry and the art market, it can sometimes be useful to have more than one seller working in partnership. One person operates as the so-called 'expert'. This is the diamond technician, or someone advising on what looks good, what not to wear, or, in the case of art, the history of the artist. It is important that the technical salesperson is divorced from closing the deal. They do not need to talk about money – they are there to advise.

Salesperson number two can then take on the role of the closer. 'Did you find my colleague helpful?' They can explore the price categories and what might suit their customer's budget.

If both sides of the sales partnership are working together consciously, each will acknowledge what the other has contributed and will say that they were equally responsible for the deal. In a less cooperative situation that acknowledgement will not be forthcoming.

Business lesson: Keeping an eye on the bottom line

When you're selling a product that is unique and variable, such as art or crafts, it can be hard to remember that the aim is still to make a profit and that the profit margin is still the key to business success.

Week 6: Advertising
Marketing and branding

Advertising for Amstrad needs a certain style. We are straightforward in approach, with no need for fancy punchlines or catchy jingles, so on balance we tend to create our own adverts in house. Our advertising style reflects my own style: it tends to be straightforward and 'in your face'.

Advertising companies make little money from media-selling these days – that's all done via the media buyers. They win by charging for their creative skills. We prefer to work with our own ideas. As the technology has become easier to use, we decided that we could do our own advertisements – with the right technical partners – so we sit with the technicians and create what we want.

What does marketing mean exactly? It is the opposite of direct selling and is more to do with brand awareness or with making the public aware of the product. If you are a manufacturer, dependent upon a retailer to sell your product, marketing is about making it easier for that retailer to sell your product.

There are many companies that focus on building a brand. Amstrad has never adopted that approach. How would we market the brand? 'Always Innovating', offering products that are 'Best Value for Money' and 'Packed Full of Features' – but our products change. Our marketing is therefore much more about building awareness of our products.

There are no big marketing budgets in electronics because the products have a relatively short lifespan and therefore a slim profit margin, compared with something like baked beans, for example. If a product such as baked beans makes a tremendous profit margin, there will be financial resources available to run a periodic and probably costly advertising campaign just to remind the public that the brand is still out there, even though, generally speaking, the sales curve remains safe and steady.

Sports products have a different pricing model and are interesting for a different reason. Here the unit cost of production is very low but the vast percentage of the budget goes on marketing – the reason being that in order to sell the product, the manufacturers need to build brand awareness. The only way to do this is via continuous and costly advertising.

Electronic products rarely command the kind of margin that justifies a large marketing budget. If the product has only a certain sales volume, therein lies the profit margin and the budget for promoting it. At Amstrad we design our advertising in house and we keep it simple, focusing on features and value-for-money pricing.

I was interested to see what the teams would put together for this task and to see whether they would remember basic commercial principles or get carried away in a storm of creativity.

> 'Advertising: one of my favourite, favourite things.
> I've written books on advertising. You might not
> have found them for sale on the Internet because
> they're cheque books – big fat cheque books!'
>
> **SIR ALAN**

Task 6: Creating an advertising campaign

GOAL: To produce an advertising campaign
CHALLENGE: To establish an instant market for a never-before-seen product. To think of how to pitch a campaign, design and present it

Rules and regulations
- The teams were briefed and asked to design an ad campaign for a new product.
- Each team had a budget of £1000.
- They briefed themselves on the product by trying to use it, and worked out the possible markets it was aimed at.
- At a minimum, they had to produce one print advert and a 30-second television advert.
- The teams presented the campaign proposal: the strongest campaign would win.

Skills tested
- Evaluating a complex brief.
- Imagination in coming up with new ideas.
- Understanding of the market.
- Pitching an idea.
- Communicating an idea to professional creatives.

Evaluating a complex brief
When faced with a brief it is important to **decide what the priorities are**, and in business that's easy. It's finance – starting with the budget. In turn, the budget is driven by the bottom line. If we are selling a specific item that has a fashionable shelf-life of, say, 18 months, we've got to sell a certain quantity

over that period. The quantity that we sell has to equate to a gross margin, and that gross margin will let you know how much you've got left for your advertising budget. Simple really, but not all our candidates saw it that way.

Imagination in coming up with new ideas

A lot of people think of themselves as creative, and brainstorming is a favourite occupation in most organizations. The challenge comes when you are surrounded by 100 different ideas and have to decide which of them has 'legs'. If you are running a theme through a variety of different media, **it is important to ensure that the central concept has a simplicity** and clarity for the punters to understand. We had a number of creative thinkers among our teams, but the challenge was to keep the ideas grounded in order to convey the central message.

Understanding of the market

An advert needs to convey the right message to the market sector that is actually going to purchase the product. Children's advertising is probably the most blatant, telling you what the features of the products are, how much fun it's going to be to play with and how much it costs. Advertising is so often a self-indulgence. I get irritated by watching adverts that are meaningless, and so far removed from the product they are selling to convey information. Advertising has become an art form in its own right – and an entertainment. Presumably, companies with big budgets get a return on their investment, but in some instances, frankly, I'd be surprised. In my world we keep it simple: we identify who'll buy the product and we speak to them directly and in a way that informs.

There were some bright people on our teams with some solid sales experience, so I was pretty confident that they would keep their objective in mind. The results were very interesting.

Pitching an idea
Advertising has a very short period in which to make an impact. It is usually the repetition of exposure that hooks the buyer. If the person with the concept can sell it, and get others to buy into it, then it is likely to fly. With so many creative players around the table, I was interested to find out who listened to whom and how they reached team consensus regarding a marketable concept.

Communicating an idea to professional creatives
Professional creatives are a crucial part of your team. They are among the first people who truly need to buy into your concept. If they don't get it, either change your designer (early on) or, if you respect the professional's opinion, think again.

It is important to remember that designers, typographers and photographers are talented people who have skills that you don't have. They also have a visual sense that will bring something extra to the table – but it is still not their project. **Designers need space to be creative**, but need your guidance to ensure that the look works for the marketplace. My advice would always be not to move too far away from your designer, and to keep yourself involved in the process. **Mistakes can be expensive**, and that cost is coming off your bottom-line profit.

Danger point: Negotiating with a jobs-worth
It's very rare these days to have main dealings with someone who is at a sufficiently senior level to have the complete view, so it is usually middle management that you come up against. It is rare at that level to find someone who will take risks.

In order to deal effectively with jobs-worths and blockers, it's important to pre-empt and overcome the obstacles in their minds. Build them a big fat comfort-pillow on which to make a decision; then you'll have them onside. Don't ask them to take risks, because your competitors may come along later and be more ready to bend to their rules, which will leave them with the commercial advantage.

Business lesson: Managing difficult people

Personality clashes are a fact of life. I don't expect to like everyone I work with, and I don't expect everyone who works for me to like each other, but I do expect them to work together in an effective and professional manner.

If communication breaks down, or tempers flare, the business suffers. If the differences are irreconcilable, I take a good hard look at the individuals' personal qualities and do what I can to keep them apart. Of course, if one of those people is rubbing a lot of staff up the wrong way, I have a problem, and that person has to go.

Week 7: **People management**
Charity fund-raising

Like many people in the public eye, I am approached daily with requests for money, appearances and various other favours. Many of them get filed in the dustbin. Spreading money thinly just doesn't work. Giving a large donation to a single charity is more effective than giving small amounts to several. But I am careful to make sure that 80 per cent of the donation isn't spent on supporting the infrastructure of the charity.

There are many thousands of wannabe Apprentices who would have walked 100 miles to take part in the next task facing the teams, just for the opportunity of meeting celebrities. But what appears to be a glamorous job on the surface usually represents a great deal of extremely hard work behind the scenes – as our teams were about to find out.

The real task here was to **handle people effectively**. Celebrities are people who are in the public eye a great deal and whose larger-than-life personalities can need careful handling. They are people who can spot a time-waster at 100 yards, who are approached on a regular basis by people who want things from them. Celebrities are often under a great deal of pressure themselves.

Having gained the attention of their celebrities, our intrepid Apprentices then had to convince them to participate in the task.

How should you handle a celebrity?
When speaking to someone who is bombarded daily with requests, to have their attention at all means that you are 70 per cent there. The Apprentices

had to watch the body language, however, to make sure they had the celebrities' attention and were not irritating them.

In general the guidelines are:
- Crank up the sales pitch if you are talking to a 'soft' person.
- Go into 'listening' mode if speaking to a tougher customer.
- Be yourself.

I am often confronted with people who feel they need to imitate what they perceive to be my gruffness of approach when they want something from me. They will adopt an aggressive and belligerent manner, which, frankly, will get them nowhere fast. **Play-acting annoys me** at the best of times, but this 'wide-boy' approach irritates me most of all. Anyone with an aggressive attitude is kicked out immediately. People who gain my attention tend to **get to the point** as quickly as possible, are logical, honest and straightforward. The same principles will apply to most people.

'I need closers! I need doers!'

SIR ALAN

Task 7: Fund-raising for a charity

GOAL: To persuade celebrities to make contributions towards a fund-raising event

CHALLENGE: To negotiate, organize and deliver

Rules and regulations

- The two team leaders were presented with a list of celebrities.
- The teams researched their celebrities and discovered what they might offer. They had to schedule meetings and meet their celebrities face-to-face to negotiate for their time.
- They chaperoned their celebrities to the venue, and the winning team was the one that raised the most money.

Skills tested

- Negotiation.
- Diplomacy.
- Charm under pressure.
- Ability to add value.
- Organization.
- Delegation.

Negotiation

Negotiating with someone in the public eye is no different from negotiating with anyone anywhere else. However, acute attention to the person's body language is needed, and, owing to time constraints, it is important to be well prepared and aim to close the discussion with an agreed action as quickly as possible.

Diplomacy

Tactfulness is always important, and those in the public eye are likely to reject inappropriate, downright rude or ill-informed approaches. **Be polite. Be sensitive. Be clear. Be honest.** You will get a far better response.

Charm under pressure

Celebrities have, in the main, turned charm under pressure into a professional skill. You may feel as if you are under pressure, but it is nothing compared to their experience of being constantly in the public eye, so **keep calm and keep smiling**.

Ability to add value

The art of selling includes being able to add value to the simplest item. If the item has belonged to a celebrity, that is your added value. It is important to **understand the value of what you are selling** and what your market will pay for it. If you have a wealthy audience who have come to spend money, the value of the goods you are selling needs to match the expectations and lifestyle of your audience.

Organization

Plan your task. Plan how you would like it to go. If you are the team leader, communicate the plan to your team and ensure you have their support and backing. Once these preparations are in place, **make at least one contingency plan** because when you're dealing with other people – especially celebrities – nothing ever goes entirely as you expect it to.

Delegation

Bear in mind that whatever the task, it is always important for each member of the team to **know what is expected** of them and to act accordingly. Acting as a team does not mean doing everything together; that just leads to confusion.

Danger point: Thinking small

When speaking to famous people, there can be a tendency for awe of their fame to get in the way and make you miss the opportunity of gaining the 'big prize'. It's important to know who you are speaking to, to listen carefully to what they are saying and to recognize both their 'market value' and what the general public most values about them. If you have got as far as winning the interest of someone whose fame can help raise funds, there is little point in using the opportunity to gain something you could have achieved without their input.

Business lesson: Effective briefing

When selling through a third party, whether a salesperson, a retailer or an auctioneer, it is crucially important to remember that yours is unlikely to be the only product they are selling. A salesperson rarely has longer than three minutes to make a pitch, and frequently has to make a positive sales impact with a single sentence. It is up to the individual briefing the salesperson to ensure that they understand the unique selling point of the item and that they have been given a helpful one-liner with which to sell it.

Week 8: Margins
Controlling your costs

One of the most important aspects of any business is to **keep an eye on costs.** Monthly, even weekly, I check that we are covering our costs and that we are selling our goods at the right price. This is the single most important thing in our business.

We make sure that we are keeping the costs of our materials down to the level we have planned for, and that our overheads and manufacturing costs are not running away with themselves. If they are increasing in cost, we have to increase our prices (which does not happen very often, I might add).

This task tested the ability of the Apprentices to keep their eye on the bottom line.

Key questions to ask
- What is the product?
- Which product will sell the best?
- What kind of pricing do you want to sell the product for?
- What kind of margin are you looking for?
- How much are you going to spend on organization?

The amount you have to spend on manufacturing the product is determined by what's left over from your organization costs.

I know it sounds too easy when put like that, but it really is that simple; and yet you would be amazed at how many people start at the wrong end of the process, or just don't see it at all.

At Amstrad the first thing we establish when we set out to make a product is how much we can sell it for. If the team considers that the top-end price is £99, there you have it – the first stake in the ground. From that point you work backwards to calculate your ideal margin, VAT, dealer margin, the cost of designing and building a prototype, production and overheads. Once you've stripped all that out, what's left is the amount you have to spend on materials. Simple.

If you go about it the wrong way round and focus on design first and costs afterwards, you are a slave to price – and whether you price high or low, you will still lose a load of money. I'd be watching out for that on this task.

The bottom line is: **if you cannot afford to buy the components, you can't afford to make the product.** In an ideal world I would create a car that runs on water and sell it for £1000 a time, but it's just not possible. In the electronics business you can't afford to make a product that is feature-less. In a farmers' market you won't get repeat business if you produce a product that is flavourless. You need to be aware that with any idea you might get to a point where you just have to walk away.

'Always start off with a target profit
margin in mind. Without focusing on
that you are dead in the water.'

SIR ALAN

Task 8: Maximizing profits at a farmers' market

GOAL: To add value to agricultural produce and create a food product for sale
CHALLENGE: To make the maximum margin

Rules and regulations
- The teams had to research, develop and manufacture food product(s) for sale.
- Each team had seed money of £750.
- They had to source and buy their raw ingredients.
- They had to process, brand and package the produce to increase its value.
- They had to supply full accounts and paperwork for this task on the sheets provided.

Skills tested
- Sourcing.
- Exercising cost control.
- Researching competitors.
- Pricing.
- Maximizing profit margins.

We had a lot of experience of catering across the teams of Apprentices, so this task was going to be an interesting mix of general ability combined with expertise.

The challenge on this occasion was not to maximize takings, but to make the largest **profit margin – that critical space between cost of sales**

and turnover. There was also the challenge of dealing with lots of goods that would quickly exceed their sell-by date.

The big temptation when entering the food industry is to treat catering the way you would a dinner party. You want the best for your guests and you want everyone to compliment you and come back for more. This is all well and good, but in the commercial world you need to make sure that the reason people are coming back for more is down to good value and good quality, rather than superior quality for the price and too much value for money.

Effective stock control is crucial. Simplicity is essential. Too many product lines can be a mistake, and it is also important not to spend too much on your basic ingredients.

Danger point: Deciding on your budget

Buying ingredients or materials without first deciding what your profit margin should be is rather like going on a shopping spree without checking your bank balance first. It is a high-risk strategy. Budget is crucial.

Business lesson: Margin is king

As elsewhere in business, profit margin is king in catering. The place to check for potential profit is not in the day's takings, but in the amount of food that is wasted. Would our Apprentices grasp this crucial point?

Week 9: Direct selling
The challenge of selling face to face

This was the greatest challenge to date for our six remaining Apprentices. If you were faced with a captive audience of 36,000 people, how would you grab their attention? This assignment was described as marketing, but it was, in fact, a challenging face-to-face sales task. The solutions our Apprentices came up with were inventive, creative and took a lot of thought and planning.

The problem with advertising – in print or on TV – is that it costs a great deal because you have to place ads consistently. This ensures they enter consumer consciousness gradually, irrevocably, over a long period of time. On average, it takes three or four airings for a consumer to notice an advert. Leaflets are all very well. They are useful for making paper aeroplanes, for example! Punters will often take a leaflet from a vendor because it's easier than saying no and walking away.

The key point here was that a group of people who had paid money to have a good time, at the event where the task took place, were in a positive mood. They wanted things to go well. They were feeling optimistic. They were in just the frame of mind to be sold to. Our Apprentices had something to sell and they had the customers in the palm of their hands.

How do you sell to them? You connect with them. Talk, talk, talk – you **don't stop talking**. One team member in particular did rather a lot of that!

Careful planning, knowing your product and the competition and targeting the customer with **the right information is crucial** when selling direct.

If you are looking for high value, you need to target the right sector of people, and make sure you make their decision easy. If your own business is dependent upon sales and you have direct contact with your customers, my advice would be stay with them face to face until the deal is made. Marketing material has great value, but is at its most effective when you are there to pitch it to them – so keep talking!

Implicit in this direct face-to-face selling task was the need to keep an eye on how things were going. When you have only nine hours to achieve results, you need to remain very flexible. You need to assess what is working, and to change tack fast if you think you are not getting results. But to do that you need to **keep an eye on your sales progress** during the selling period, and **alter your tactics quickly** if you are not getting the sales.

'In football you see players that look very busy, running in, and out, tackling, dribbling, falling over, getting up … There's a lot of dancing going on, but where's the end product?'

SIR ALAN

Task 9: Marketing a product

GOAL: To set up a stall at a major public location and get people to sign up to a mobile phone subscription service

CHALLENGE: To sell services with no visible product while under time pressure

Rules and regulations

- The teams had to sign up new customers.
- Each team had to design a competition and/or promotion to attract subscribers, erect a stand in the building concourse and obtain uniforms.
- Each team had £2000 seed money.
- The teams were responsible for ensuring that their plans abided by health and safety regulations.
- The winning team was the one that obtained the most subscriptions.

Skills tested

- Entrepreneurial flair.
- Ability to persuade customers to sign.
- Remaining calm in high-pressure conditions.
- Optimizing a location.
- Teamwork.

Entrepreneurial flair

Each of the candidates had entrepreneurial flair, but which of them would cope best with face-to-face pressure on the day, combined with cold weather and a host of other challenges? You need to be inventive and persistent when faced with a large crowd of people. You need to **grab attention and add the entertainment factor**. This task brought out the best and the worst in our candidates. There were some very inventive and effective marketing ideas on the table. The candidates I expected to shine did not necessarily rise to the occasion; others became hungry for a win and cut right to the chase in order to achieve their objective.

Ability to persuade customers to sign
Slick talk and long-term marketing plans are all very well, but we were looking for sign-ups on the day. How would the candidates plan their attack? How would they prioritize the markets to focus on? How well would they operate as a team? And, face to face with the customer, would the Apprentices be able to **clinch the sale** on the spot or let the deal slip away?

Remaining calm in high-pressure conditions
Panic spreads, so in any business situation self-discipline is the order of the day. Feeling out of your depth? Use the feeling as motivation to get better informed. Having an off-day? Focus on lifting your team-mates so that their positive enthusiasm pulls you through. One of our candidates in particular was not at their best and confessed to some personal issues. The question was, did this affect the overall team performance? It's always a difficult call. Frustrated that the best-laid plans have gone awry? I've said it before – always expect things to go wrong and **have a contingency plan**. Success is about taking risks, but not about leaving yourself vulnerable to defeat. This assignment proved to be about more than just the task in hand.

Optimizing a location
It pays to know your territory, and to know where your competition is based. I was very interested to see the decisions the teams took and why.

Teamwork

Some of our more astute Apprentices realized very early on that the only way to avoid going to the boardroom, with its threat of being fired, was to **put ego to one side** and concentrate on delivering the task in hand as part of a team. By task 9 our contenders knew each other's strengths and weaknesses quite well, but would that mean they could work together effectively as a team? It can be very difficult to communicate when you are split up on site, so careful planning, a clear strategy and effective delegation would be important. Several of the Apprentices cited this task as the most difficult of all.

Danger point: Stonewallers

This task wasn't without its challenges. In every organization there are people who take decisions that may not be theirs to make. This may be because they have not been fully briefed by senior management or it may be because they are concerned by something that is a threat to their business at that particular point in time, or it may just be that they have a tendency towards self-importance. There is often no clear answer – but a stonewaller can cause frustration. There is no point in trying to deflate them; they will just dig their heels in deeper. In general, it is true to say that everything is negotiable, but on occasion you may come up against someone who simply doesn't want to shift their position. In that case, recognize that you are not going to get anywhere and change your tactics. Always have a contingency plan.

Business lesson: Flexibility

When you're out in the field your project management needs to be sound because communication can be difficult. The project manager has to be very well prepared, brief the team, be observant and be very ready to listen and react if things are going wrong.

Week 10: Sales presentation
An electronic trip to the market

In the past, television has been a critical selling tool, but with so many TV channels now available, its power has been diluted tremendously. Most of the major brands do still invest in TV advertising, so one has to assume it still works, but it is no longer the be all and end all. The amount of money that is required to advertise on television is awesome, so this task – to sell on TV – was an important one.

Until recently, TV adverts were designed as short interruptions to programmes. With the advent of satellite TV there is now an expanded opportunity for advertising. It says a lot about the public that there is a new breed of TV channel, that relies *solely* on selling products. I suppose it's a kind of electronic trip to the market, but instead of wandering around the stalls or shops you can simply flick through lots of shopping channels, buying if you want to, and switching off if you don't. This sort of electronic mail-order catalogue can work, but the user really needs to have the desire specifically to tune into such a channel. You've got to like shopping – I mean *really* like shopping – and this must tell you something about the people who watch.

Selling on television requires presentation skills rather than media skills. It's important to **present yourself well** because you're launching a product and giving a presentation to a group of customers. It's also vital how you present the information about the product – there's no point in waffling, **time is money**! You have to know exactly what the **unique selling point** of your product is and get that message across quickly and clearly. The buyer needs to know what features will be of relevance to him or her. How is it special? Why do they want it? How will it enhance their lives?

Presenting a sales pitch can be nerve-wracking. The pressure of performing for an audience is high octane. You not only need the accurate information to present, but you also need the confidence and ability to perform.

To give a good presentation you need to:

- Learn by doing.
- Anticipate questions that could be asked.
- Make sure you are looking in the right direction and not confuse people by giving mixed messages.
- Realize that timing is important.

I wanted to see how the Apprentices presented themselves as well as the product; whether they were effective in closing a sale; how well they coped in front of the camera; and whether they were clear and concise or garbled. If they had the main ingredients, I would overlook imperfections.

'Fair? Fair? Listen, we don't do fair here. The only
fare you'll get here is your bloody train fare home!'

SIR ALAN

Task 10: Presenting a sales pitch

GOAL: To sell under time pressure to unseen customers
CHALLENGE: Tactical selling on a TV sales channel

Rules and regulations
- Each team received training in the art of media sales.
- The team members were given a choice of products.
- Each team had half an hour to sell three products. Each product
  carried a target price. The idea was to meet or exceed it.
- The team with the highest profit was the winner.

Skills tested
- Ability to select the right products for the marketplace.
- Teamwork.
- Ability to hit sales targets.
- Ability to cope with pressure.
- Evolving a sales pitch that holds attention.
- Knowing when to change tack.

The skills used for this task were similar to those needed for previous tasks, but
their application was different. Selecting the right products for the market the
Apprentices were trying to reach, would be an important element to this task.

Teamwork
The teams were small and working together tightly on this occasion. Coordinated and clear **teamwork was critical** in getting the the right details at
the right time to get the message across to the home audience. This was a
great task, as I could take part from the comfort of my own home!

Ability to hit sales targets
Selling via a television sales channel is a bit like being a puppet on a string: your team-mates are guiding your actions and you need to be ready to **transform yourself** at a moment's notice. You may be selling cheese one minute, clothing fabric the next, then jewellery, DIY tools … you name it. To hit the targets the presenters needed to identify the essence of the product, communicate with the audience and create a buzz, just as a street vendor does when he's selling his wares – being loud, bold and **giving customers plenty of information**.

Ability to cope with pressure
The pressure in this instance related to the speed with which the vendor had to absorb information, and the clarity with which it had to be relayed to the viewers. This was a pretty intensive activity, guaranteed to stretch each candidate's abilities in a way they had never had the opportunity to be tested before.

What interested me was how each candidate coped with the pressure – and I would say each of them handled it well on the day. Whether they would be able to **cope with the pressure** if they ended up in the boardroom was another matter … .

Evolving a sales pitch that holds attention
A successful sales pitch needs to be to the point, entertaining, appropriate, to involve the audience, and needs to **communicate**. The viewers need to be persuaded that they are being sold something that is going to improve their lives if they purchase it – in fact they need and want this product! High value goods need greater depth of description and more facts than others. No one on the team had experience of selling in this very demanding environment. They had to learn pretty fast!

Knowing when to change tack

In any sales situation – from retail selling to a corporate deal to a car boot sale – you need to know when to push and when to step away from chasing a deal. **In the true salesperson an instinct develops** and you can tell when you've got a done deal. The beauty of watching shopping channels on TV is that the sales unfold in front of your eyes. You can tell almost immediately whether you have hooked the public interest by the running total of sales being made while you are on air, and you can change tack or change product in response. Of course, for that to work you need to have chosen the right products to sell in the first place. Did our Apprentices get it right?

Danger point: Product selection

This was uncharted territory for our contestants. Few of them had ever watched a TV sales channel, and they had to learn fast. Not all products lend themselves to on-screen sales. Some are too complicated to sell, so they needed to ask some pretty astute questions of their advisers to make the right selection. Was the home audience interested in luxury holidays, DIY or food projects? Who would be watching? There were all kinds of potential pitfalls for our teams.

Business lesson: Teamwork

When the pressure is on, clarity is everything. It's critical that each individual knows what they are doing and is not overloaded with information that leaves them dazed and confused. Had the team leaders got the balance right? And who was running the show?

Week 11: Interviewing
Interviews and how to survive them

Every job interview at every level should aim to assess the following:
- Skills and experience appropriate to the business.
- Personal characteristics.
- Whether the shortlist candidates will fit the organization.
- Whether the preferred candidate has the 'wow' factor.

The Apprentices who reached this stage of the competition had been on **a fast-track business journey**. They had been tested beyond their normal limits, had overcome immense challenges, had learnt a great deal, had come to know each other very well, and had developed their team skills very effectively.

Now, however, it was up to them as individuals. Their CVs would be read, reviewed, inspected, dissected and questioned – hard. If there were any cracks, we now had enough inside knowledge of their attitude, skills and behaviour to be able to find them!

An interview is a two-way process. It is primarily about the interviewer(s) deciding whether you have the right skills, abilities and personality for their business culture. Equally, however, it is about the candidates deciding whether the role, culture and scope of the job are going to be beneficial in building their careers.

A successful interview and the ability to sell yourself draws on many of the skills outlined in Part 1 of this book. Do you think like a winner? Can you lead from the front? How hungry are you – for the job, as well as personal success? Can you sell yourself as you would any other product you believe in? Just as you would take time to get to know a product you are selling, so too you need to know yourself.

At the end of the day you are going through a formal buying and selling process, and the buyer needs to decide whether they want to keep you, or whether they will wish they'd made a different style of purchase once the deal is done.

'There's a new bloody world out there, full of spotty-faced MBAs with spreadsheets, putting obstacles in my way. They are costing me money. It's time to start recruiting people to play the new game, but direct them to focus on our old-fashioned objectives.'

SIR ALAN

Task 11: Undergoing boardroom interviews

GOAL: To be selected as one of the last two Apprentices
CHALLENGE: To survive intensive high-pressure questioning

Qualities assessed
- Intelligence.
- Ability to perform well at interviews.
- Ability to sell yourself.
- Nerves under pressure.
- Coherence.
- Suitability for the company culture.

The remaining Apprentices were put through a whole day of gruelling interviews. During these hard, tense and personal sessions, their CVs were dissected and any possible exaggerations highlighted, and their performance in previous tasks was examined.

Intelligence
In life, as in business, **there are different kinds of intelligence**. That is not meant to be philosophical; it's a simple statement of fact. A theological scholar with several degrees and diplomas is undoubtedly intelligent, but would not survive much further than the reception desk in one of our organizations! A street trader in London, Manchester or Glasgow has a different kind of savvy: they have street-smart intelligence and highly tuned survival skills – very useful in business. I was looking for someone who had the demeanour and presence to operate at a senior level, but who was street smart as well.

Whether you are interviewer or interviewee, I would recommend being absolutely honest about your corporate culture and the kind of intelligence you need before you begin the interview process.

Ability to perform well at interviews

We always talk about performing well at interviews, and there's no doubt that in many cases the performance can be greater than the substance! What is needed is not a false façade that the interviewers then have to unpeel like a many-layered parcel, but clarity, honesty and well-prepared and calm presentation. The interviewers are not there to get to know you as a friend would over a long period of time; they need to be able to assess quickly whether you would be good for the commercial future of the organization.

The Internet, dozens of books and myriad courses exist to tell you the obvious:

- Make sure you have researched the company before you attend the interview. They are taking the trouble to read about you, and you are of no interest to them if you don't know who they are or why you're there.
- Look smart. You are being judged. It doesn't matter that everyone else in the company is walking around in jeans and trainers. You are there to sell something invaluable – you are there to sell yourself.
- When you go into a shop and you're making a purchase, do you buy the product in the damaged box, or do you hunt for the one in pristine packaging? It doesn't matter that, damaged or undamaged, either box will go straight into the bin once you get home, nor that the product inside the damaged box is exactly the same

as the one in the pristine box. You are making an investment and you want perfection. Employers are the same. They are looking for the perfect candidate. If you haven't ironed your shirt, or your shoes are down at heel, they will wonder what else you are likely to neglect in business.

- Speak clearly and slow down: you need to be heard as well as understood. If you bombard your interviewer with too much information at once, they will be overwhelmed and have to work too hard to ensure they have understood your core strengths. Look at the person you are speaking to and ensure that you are giving each other undivided attention.

- Be aware of the characteristics required for the role you are applying for, and be ready to talk about your strengths, your weaknesses and your personal achievements in life in relation to the skills the interviewer is looking for.

- Have the courage to be yourself at all times.

Ability to sell yourself

It is important to be able to **give a good account of yourself** in life – not just at interview, but when operating in business both generally and socially. As mentioned earlier, this does not mean putting on an act, but it does mean presenting a **confidence and self-assurance** that others can rely on. You have to know your skills and know yourself. I'm not recommending years of psychotherapy here, although there's nothing wrong in that if it's needed; I simply mean that the more you are true to yourself, the more you will be believed, and the more likely you are to get the job. After that, the normal rules of selling apply: **keep it focused, keep it clear, keep to the point.**

Nerves under pressure

I see adrenalin as a good thing. Adrenalin is what feeds your energy levels and provides a sense of urgency in life. Usually, the only time adrenalin really becomes detrimental in an interview situation is when a candidate is badly prepared.

Of course, some interviewers adopt very direct tactics, and more senior-level interviews can be extremely intense and personal. The thing to do is not to take them personally. You are there to inform the interviewer, and they are there to decide whether you and your skills are right for the job they are offering. **It is a buying and selling process – it's not personal!**

Coherence

It is amazing how many people will begin to babble incoherently when they feel they are in the spotlight. **Stop. Pause. Think.** Before answering any question, ensure that you know why it is being asked, and the likely impact of your answer. Coherence is critical to making a strong impression. It implies self-assurance, intelligent thinking, an ability to think on your feet, and calmness under pressure.

Suitability for the company culture

Once again, it comes down to **research in advance** of the interview itself. Find out as much as you can. If you don't like what you see, don't waste anyone's time. However, if you're potentially interested and have further questions, or you're ecstatic about the opportunity and are desperate for the job, do your research and, in the words of your average boy scout, 'be prepared'.

Danger points: False pretences and favouritism

As a candidate, trying to be someone you are not is always a major mistake. Never say things just to impress.

As an interviewer, deciding purely on the basis of personality is always a mistake. If you are tempted to choose someone simply because you like their company, seek a second opinion because you are likely to be blind to some of their faults.

Business lesson: Listen to advice

As a candidate, the best way to be hired is to be well prepared, and to be aware of what you can bring to the company in both the commercial and personal sense.

As an interviewer, never ask for advice unless you are willing to listen to it, and always ask the advice of those you trust. Add the knowledge of others to your own knowledge and experience, and make an informed decision, not an impulsive one. Although it sounds contradictory, it is much easier to fire people before you hire them – that is, before they have become part of your team!

Week 12: Event management
The art of planning and leadership

This task was the culmination of 12 weeks' intensive effort. A business journey unlike any other, it allowed our intrepid Apprentices to develop skills, try new business areas, develop their management and leadership skills, and demonstrate to me that they had what it takes to make it within one of my organizations.

In the final event, each of our two finalists was on their own. The business planning and decisions were up to them as individuals. There was no more 'we'; now it was all 'I, me, my' in a test of leadership, project management, time management, financial acumen and decision-making ability. This task was pure **business at the sharp end**.

While I would love to include a section here that tells you all about the final outcome, we don't want to ruin your surprise when you watch the programme. The issues that came up and the challenges that our two finalists had to overcome were not dissimilar to those that take place in every office across the country every day. The location was different, but not the issues involved.

'It's not just about money and profit this time … I will be looking at your man-management skills and customer satisfaction, as well as your past performance … It's not going to be easy.'

SIR ALAN

Task 12: Project managing an event

GOAL: To successfully organize and manage an event
CHALLENGE: To project manage the event from start to finish, and to brief and motivate a personally chosen team

Rules and regulations
- The last two Apprentices each had two days to plan an up-market event, recruit all necessary staff and design a venue.
- They had two days trying to fill the venue with fee-paying guests.
- They had £5000 seed money.
- The event had to have food, drink, entertainment and a recognizable theme.
- Candidates would be judged on their overall success in managing all aspects of this project: logistics, budget, promotion and marketing of the event, customer satisfaction, staff management, creativity and profitability.
- The winner was the candidate who made the most money.

Skills tested
- Business management.
- People management.
- The art of delegation.
- Communication.
- Leadership.

The previous tasks provide a run-down of the key skills and abilities that are needed in order to be successful in business. When it comes to event management the key factors are as follow.

Business management
- Vision – clearly defined and easily communicated.
- Planning – every aspect of the project broken into manageable tasks.
- Networking – who do you know who can help you deliver your idea? Involve them from the early stages and make sure they feel appreciated.
- Budgeting – start with your target price, your necessary profit margin and work back to costs.
- Implementation – through effective delegation and third-party expertise.
- Marketing – to make your market aware that you have something they will want to buy.
- Selling – the cornerstone of success. Without effective sales you will not deliver a successful project.
- Delivery – in the case of an event, delivery is in two main stages:
  1. Delivering the project to launch.
  2. Ensuring that your paying guests have the time of their lives.

People management
- Motivating – especially your trusted inner team, who will then, in turn, motivate others.
- Delegating – once you have drawn up your plan, delegate as much as possible to able people whom you can trust to deliver.
- Communicating – clearly, directly and frequently. Keep in touch throughout the process and make sure all is on track.

- Leading – from the front and with confidence, even if your style is instinctively consensual. Unless you show leadership you will not command respect, and unless you command respect you will not be kept properly informed.

How do you motivate your team? When you're on a limited budget, pay can seem like a major hurdle to achieving your ends, but the truth is, contrary to popular belief, pay is not the main motivator in people's choice of work; there are many non-financial incentives as well:

- Quality of work.
- A need to belong as part of a team.
- A sense of achievement.
- Recognition of success and effort.
- The opportunity to progress in career.
- Personal fulfilment.
- Increased responsibility and autonomy.

All of these are cheaper than a pay rise and can add a great deal to the effectiveness of a project.

A successful team wants to like its leader; the individuals enjoy sharing in the success of the team and will spark new ideas that will lead to a more financially successful business.

The art of delegation

Delegation, as I have said before, is not about letting go; it is about planning in advance and communicating throughout. Delegation is the equivalent of a brain extension. You are using someone else's brain to deliver your thoughts. So don't fall asleep on the job. **You can't deliver if you're not concentrating** – even with all the brains at your disposal!

Communicating for success

Communication is not about breathing down everyone's necks, nor is it about waiting to be told. Communication is about using your nose to sense what might go wrong before it happens and to see it off at the pass; it is about keeping in touch with your key players and ensuring that they share your vision, are on side and are delegating effectively themselves; it is also about being seen by the rest of the people involved in the project, being available if required for important issues, and keeping everyone informed in practical terms about what is going on. Save the flattery and the niceties for later. Acknowledge and appreciate when people have delivered, but keep things moving.

Leading from the front

It is human nature to want a role model, and to want to work for someone you respect. Never underestimate what you are teaching people about yourself and about management when you are in a leadership role. For good or bad, you will be judged and assessed, so you may as well **be a confident, motivating and well-organized leader** that your team can respect rather than one who is remembered forever for incompetence and ingratitude.

Event management is incredibly challenging because you are dealing with people en masse, who have paid to have a good time. There will be divas, drunkards, acrimonious couples, and everybody's uncle, as well as party-goers, grandmothers, birthday girls and wedding parties. You will have to deal with the vagaries of the weather, the challenges presented by caterers, drivers, domestic staff and probably the police too if things get out of hand!

I had no doubt that the task would stretch the Apprentices to the utmost and, likewise, no doubt that they had the ability to deliver. It was a spectacular task and one that was a credit to all involved. No matter who I appointed to help run one of my companies, I was quite certain that both final contestants were outstanding individuals who would go far.

CONCLUSION

Fired or hired?

Firing people is not pleasant. You'd be an iron-cold person if you said it doesn't matter. Whether someone has been with the company for two weeks or 20 years, it's never easy telling them they've got to go. There are times when it's actually heartbreaking to deliver that news, but it has to be done. It's business, not personal.

On the other hand, there are certain types of people I have no trouble firing: the lazy, the incompetent, the disloyal ….

Before shooting began on *The Apprentice* I was sure I would find it difficult to say 'I'm sorry, you're fired' to at least one of the Apprentices. I was also convinced that it would be delightful to say 'You're fired' to one or more of them. However, I knew that we would get to a situation, especially at the end, when those words would be heartbreaking, not necessarily for me, but for the Apprentice. But the nature of this exercise was that one of the finalists had to go.

I was looking forward to the moment when instead of saying 'You're fired' I could say …

'You're hired!'

A final word …

When I was starting out I was on my own. I had no mentor, no guidance, nothing. It was sheer hard work. But a successful entrepreneur cannot survive in isolation. It's important to know who your business partners are and who's in your support team. I began to employ staff when the operation became too big – when it became necessary to provide warehousing, production and packaging that I had no time or inclination to do myself.

Any young person today who feels they want to start a business on their own and wants to deal with products that cost a lot to develop and a lot to manufacture, won't be able to go it alone – it's as simple as that. It's a fact of modern life. It's my view that before you set up on your own it is important to get some commercial experience. Once you've worked for somebody and have decided whether or not you like that work, you'll be closer to understanding the industry and seeing the opportunities that exist within it.

Once you've settled down to doing what you like, and have acquired some experience, at that point only will you say, 'I tell you what – I'm going to do this for myself'. So before you leap out of bed one Monday morning shouting, 'I want to run my own airline', take the time to understand what running an airline means. Take the time to understand the industry infrastructure, see if you like it, see whether you have a desire for it, and only then begin to think about running the show yourself.

That's what happened to me. As a kid I was always interested in electronics, and I would buy crystal sets from a shop in Hackney. I suppose the tape-recorder company I first worked for attracted me because I already had an interest and an understanding. When I first started my business making amplifiers and hi-fi units it was literally a cottage industry. I made them in my garage or workshop. That was the way things happened in those days. Michael Dell, too, started off by assembling computers in his garage. But that's not possible now. If you want to be competitive in the marketplace, you have to come in with the leading-edge technology. There are no

longer any Stanley Kalms (now Lord Kalms) or Jack Cohens in the retail trade. There are very few people like me around either. It's a new wave, a new world.

Although it's more difficult these days, there are ways of getting there eventually. **Experience is the key**.

The UK is no longer a country of manufacturers. We're traders (we've always been traders), we have service-industry organizations, and, unfortunately, over the last 10 to 15 years we've seen people able to make money out of nothing, out of vapourware, out of talk, out of expectation rather than product. It has been demoralizing sometimes for a hardworking person like Arnold Weinstock, who founded GEC, to suddenly see a dot.com company come to the marketplace out of nowhere and within minutes have a market capitalization far larger than his company's. Although demoralizing, it also tells a story. It tells a story of the marketplace that you're dealing with, it tells a story of what the market is about, and it tells a story of how we have adapted dangerously towards investing in hype. The danger is that more companies will be hyped up, expectations will be hyped up, and profits don't seem to mean anything any more. Traditional ways of making money are becoming meaningless now.

The old-fashioned trader, the old-style manufacturer has gone from this country, and I suppose you've got to be realistic and understand it. At my age I find that very difficult to accept, but I recognize it and try to deal with it. I do so by employing young people to run the businesses for me.

People younger than me understand the people we're interfacing with, who we're either trying to buy from or sell to. They can enjoy playing the game, but get from me, I hope, the instinct for when to go in for the kill. They can have 17 meetings with 15 people, sit and listen to the nonsense, talk about the spreadsheets, discuss the theory, but at the end of the day, what we want is an order. At the end of the day, what we want is to buy or sell something. Unfortunately, it's not quite as simple as it was 35 years ago, and to get those goals I've had to learn to be far more patient.

Starting a business on your own is a great challenge. In my case, I just set out to be independent. It is the **small businesses** up and down the country, employing anything from two to 20 people, who **are the true backbone of the country**. There are some great success stories in Britain, and we need a lot more.

There is nothing more satisfying than **the euphoria of success**, that first week in which you earn more than you ever did when you worked for someone else. And when you employ someone, you are serving the country's economy as well as yourself.

You need to **start a business as young as you possibly can**, before you get yourself too committed with mortgages or children, and while you can still afford to take the gamble and see whether you can make it out there on your own. You must have a gambling instinct and be adventurous. You can afford to while you're young. Later on, when you have commitments, being adventurous is irresponsible. **So be bold. If you're thinking about it, do it! Set a target date!**

Only you will understand the buzz that comes from achieving something on your own. In a funny way, the money takes second place, and **what I've found really interests me now, is helping others on their way.**

You be the interviewer

Can you assess key personal characteristics and business performance to judge which Apprentice became the winner? Below is a chart that you can photocopy then fill in each week during the TV series, noting your own scores for each of the Apprentices. Transfer your total scores accumulated here each

Assess the candidates' performances each week on each of these key personal characteristics and entrepreneurial business strengths, and give them a score from 0 to 10.

	Adele	Adenike	Ben	James	
Coolness under pressure					
Courage and self-belief					
Delegation skills					
Flexibility					
Focus and decisiveness					
Gratitude towards colleagues					
Hard working					
Leadership skills					
Learning from mistakes					
Organizational skills					
Originality and forward thinking					
Planning ability					
Positive thinking					
Pro-active and action-oriented					
Self discipline					
Selling skills					
Teamworking					
Willing to seek advice					
Total scores					

week to the second chart over the page, and see how your judgement compares with that of the experts. The scores you give and the decisions you make about how well you think the Apprentices perform each task, might provide you with useful pointers about your own abilities for the future.

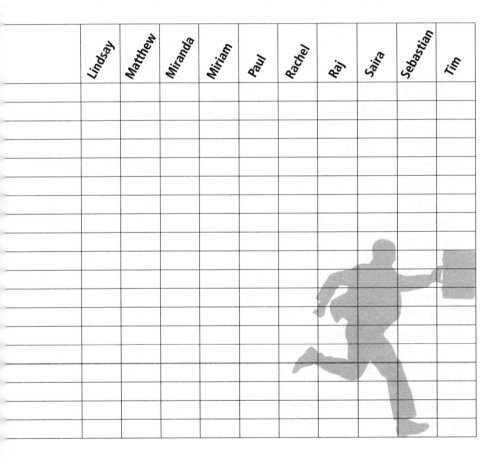

	Lindsay	Matthew	Miranda	Miriam	Paul	Rachel	Raj	Saira	Sebastian	Tim

Note your total scores for each contestant each week on this chart, then see if you've judged correctly and fired the right person!

	Adele	Adenike	Ben	James	
Task 1: Selling (14 contestants)					
Who's fired?					
Task 2: Product design (13 contestants)					
Who's fired?					
Task 3: Buying (12 contestants)					
Who's fired?					
Task 4: Retail management (11 contestants)					
Who's fired?					
Task 5: Closing the deal (10 contestants)					
Who's fired?					
Task 6: Advertising (9 contestants)					
Who's fired?					
Task 7: People management (8 contestants)					
Who's fired?					
Task 8: Controlling costs (7 contestants)					
Who's fired?					
Task 9: Direct selling (6 contestants)					
Who's fired?					
Task 10: Sales presentation (5 contestants)					
Who's fired?					
Task 11: Interviewing (4 contestants)					
Who's fired?					
Task 12: Event management (2 contestants)					
Who's fired?					
Total scores					
WHO'S HIRED?					

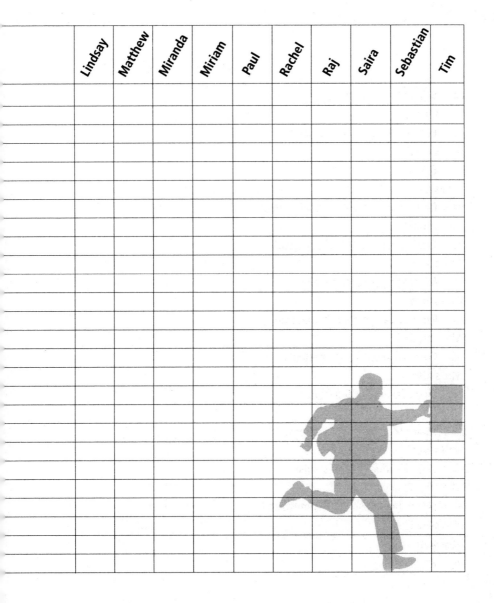

	Lindsay	Matthew	Miranda	Miriam	Paul	Rachel	Raj	Saira	Sebastian	Tim

INDEX